W9-CUY-680

THE CHURCH IS BUILT ON YOUR KNEES

The story of Pastor Pildo Joung, who has been working with God, praying to God ceaselessly, and following the guidance of the Holy Spirit

PILDO JOUNG

Translated by Rev. Eunsoo Kim, Ph.D.

Copyright © 2016 by Dr. Pildo Joung, Translated by Dr. Eunsoo Kim

The Church Is Built On Your Knees
by Dr. Pildo Joung, Translated by Dr. Eunsoo Kim

Printed in the United States of America.
Edited by Xulon Press.

ISBN 9781498470070

All rights reserved solely by the author. The author guarantees all contents are original and do not infringe upon the legal rights of any other person or work. No part of this book may be reproduced in any form without the permission of the author. The views expressed in this book are not necessarily those of the publisher.

Unless otherwise indicated, Scripture quotations taken from the New International Version (NIV). Copyright © 2011 by Biblica, Inc.™. Used by permission. All rights reserved.

www.xulonpress.com

Translator's Foreword

In His providence and grace, often God has used an ordinary man in an extraordinary way for His church and His Kingdom. Dr. Pildo Joung is one of such great servants of the Lord. He has served fifty years faithfully as a pastor.

Dr. Joung is a man of prayer. Believing "where we kneel down, there is a way," his life and ministry demonstrate "ceaseless prayers to God" and "God's answers to his prayers." He is a man of the Holy Spirit. He has been extremely sensitive to the voice of the Holy Spirit, following closely the guidance of the Holy Spirit through the words of God. He is a man of love. His life as a pastor shows how we love God, and how we love God's people as God's servants. He is truly a man of humility. Although his church became what some call a mega-church, his life demonstrates consistently the heart of a humble servant before God, confessing "everything is just by the grace of God." He is a man of vision. Since he started his pastoral ministry fifty years ago, he has had a heart aflame to bring people to our Lord. In God he has embraced a strong vision for "Evangelization of Busan, Evangelization of Korea, and Evangelization of the World." With this vision, he still visits many countries to reach people and train God's people to reach others.

While I was translating this book, very often I just stopped the work and cried out because I saw my poor Christian life as a pastor, re-examining his truly devotional life in Christ. So, very often, I had to just kneel down and repent of my sins with tears. As a missionary from Sooyoungro Church, I have had the privilege of observing Dr. Joung's life closely. This book, however, gave me a chance to see what the most important things are as a servant for Christ and what the core issues are for true Church revitalization today.

Currently, so many Churches in the world have been in serious decline. Is that simply because we are lacking in theology or certain effective pastoral skills? Regarding that question, Dr. Joung's life and ministry provide a clear direction from where we need to start as God's servants and what factors must first be recovered for true church revitalization and growth.

Pastor Eunsoo Kim, Ph.D.
President of Global Reformed Theological Seminary

Preface

God Does the Pastoral Ministry

F orty years ago[1], God built a church at Sooyoung
Rotary in Busan. The Lord, who met me in sixth grade,
set a blaze a vision for the evangelization of Korea in
my young heart and finally allowed me to plant a church
and entrusted me the mission of the "Evangelization of
Busan for Evangelization of Korea."

Since that day, the pastoral ministry of Sooyoungro
Church has been in the hands of the Lord. The Lord
has sent the people and trained them, where He led
them to missions and blessed them as well. Everything
has been accomplished in God's grace. The reason I
say this is because the pastoral ministry is operated by
the Lord, not by man; it is God Himself who makes the
church grow. The apostle Paul confirms this truth many
places in his writings.

"I planted the seed, Apollos watered it, but God has
been making it grow" (1 Cor. 3:6, NIV).

Although a church was founded by the apostle
Paul's ministry of the proclamation of the Gospel and

---

[1] This English translation used the writer's original book published in
Korea in 2005.

Apollos's ministering in the church as well, ultimately it was God who worked it to grow. It was not neither Paul nor Apollos, but it was only through the work of God.

> "So neither the one who plants nor the one who waters is anything, but only God, who makes things grow. The one who plants and the one who waters have one purpose, and they will each be rewarded according to their own labor. For we are co-workers in God's service; you are God's field, God's building" (1 Cor. 3:7-9, NIV).

It is God who makes anything grow, and men are just used by God as His servants for the work. Yet what a glorious thing to be used by God! How could we ever dare to be called "God's co-workers"?

We can see this truth in the Chinese Church. In the past, under Chinese Communism, all of the churches in China had to be closed down due to persecution and hardship. However, once the door was opened, many people have been surprised in observing the outstanding growth of the Chinese Church! No one dared to work the pastoral ministry, and for outreach, openly, but in the midst of difficult circumstances, where many risked their lives to become Christians, the Chinese Church has grown explosively. It was by the work of the Holy Spirit: it was the growth by God's sovereign plan and His providence for China. Through all of this, we are able to understand that only God has the power to work for growth.

The records of the Israelites from the exodus to the arrival of Canaan, the "land of milk and honey," demonstrate that the sovereignty of history belongs to God.

These records are not heroic stories of Moses; rather, they are the records of God leading His people to the Promised Land and training them. Also, these records give the account of Moses' process of his obedience to God. Even though the leader of the Israelites was Moses, the Bible clearly shows that it is God who allowed them to escape out of Egypt, fed them in the desert when they were starving, and gave them victories in battles against countless enemies until they entered Canaan.

Moses, simply a messenger who delivered God's commands, was a servant who obeyed God's will absolutely and was a tool revealing God's glory. When God led the Israelites with the pillars of fire and clouds, Moses and the Israelites were to simply follow them. They did not need special wisdom or power. All they needed was obedience only to God's instruction. It was God who vindicated and judged the wrongs and injustices among His people, and it was God who provided water to people with thirst. Moses' role was simply to ask God through prayer and deliver God's will to the Israelites.

Pastoral ministry today is no different. God does all things. We are just vessels used by God. All we need to do is pay attention to God and follow His leading. If we do so, I believe there will be precious fruits of God in the pastoral ministry.

With this faith, I have written this book. This faith is the consistent theme through the last forty years Sooyoungro Church history. God's sovereignty has been overflowing serenely in the journey of the forty years of Sooyoungro Church. I picked up the pen to praise the glory of God, sharing how God led someone as insufficient as myself for Sooyoungro Church.

The history of Sooyoungro Church is also the history of the Holy Spirit. In her history, there are many people of the Holy Spirit who committed themselves to fill the church with tears. With them, I would like to share the joy of the 40th Anniversary of Sooyoungro Church, and at the same time, I would like to express my heartfelt thanks to them. For the publication of this book, I would like to express my gratitude to Dr. Eunsoo Kim, President of Global Reformed Seminary and Missionary of Sooyoungro Church, for his careful work to translate this book into English. At the same time, I would like to express my gratitude to Dr. Samuel H. Larsen, Chancellor of Global Reformed Seminary, for his gracious recommendation letter for this book.Also, I would like to express my gratitude to Xulon Press for their great work to publish this book in English. Especially, I would like to express my heartfelt thanks and love to my beloved wife, Shin-Shil Park, who has faithfully served me, being committed to prayer for me as a prayer partner.

Above all, I would like to share the grace of the Church led by the Holy Spirit with many co-workers for the Lord who devoted themselves for evangelization of the world.

Table of Contents

Table of Contents

CHAPTER 1

Calling: God Ties Down The Called

The Changed Can Change the World

After twenty-six years since Sooyoungro Church was planted at Sooyoung Rotary, we experienced the joy of completing the new church building project and had a dedication service. When the building project was launched with the hope in the Lord to save 500,000 souls in the city of Busan, many said it was impossible, shaking their heads. Above all, there were eighty different landlords for the land that we were trying to purchase, and at that time, Korea was going through an economic crisis, so-called IMF cold wave. Due to all these circumstances, many expected that it would not be easy to build a new church building.

This expectation, however, was only a human thought. God gave me a clear conviction through His word in Isaiah 45:2–3:

> I will go before you and will level the
> mountains; I will break down gates of
> bronze and cut through bars of iron. I will
> give you hidden treasures, riches stored
> in secret places, so that you may know
> that I am the LORD, the God of Israel,
> who summons you by name (NIV).

Just as in the Word of God, God first built the faith of the saints in our congregation before starting the church building and allowed them to have voluntarily committed hearts. Thus, during the period of the new church building project, everyone experienced the closely guided hands of the Lord. God guided us in finishing the project without any accidents, errors, or difficulties. After the new building project was completed, not only the congregation of Sooyoungro Church, but the visitors also admired the church site. The current church site is located in the best location in an important position between Haewoondae[2] and Kwangali. The beautiful Pacific Ocean is in front of the church, and Mt. Jang, located behind the church, provides fresh air. In addition, it is very good geographically for the church because there are many apartment complexes around the church.

The new building of Sooyoungro Church, positioned in such a wonderful place and built majestically, resembles a soaring eagle high in the sky. God has done it all. I hope and pray that through this new church facility,

---

[2] Haewoondae is a beautiful beachfront community that attracts tens of thousands of tourists in all seasons. It has been subject to considerable commercial development in recent decades and is considered to be one of the most sought after residential areas in Korea.

the day of the evangelization of the city of Busan will come quickly.

However, I do not believe that God sets His eyes on Sooyoungro Church because of any external aspects of the church. In the same way, having the grand title of senior pastor at a mega-church or having the title of a successful businessman does not please the Lord. As the externals grow and become large, there is a danger of growing pride. For this reason, the faith that does not miss essentials is absolutely necessary. Thus, I preached the following message around the time we first moved to the new facility:

> A man moved to a brand new house. Though there were frequent quarrels between the husband and wife due to several problems, they decided to have a fresh start and manage a happy family life as they moved into the new house. However, the pledge did not last long. Just like before, they quarreled day and night, and as a result, their decision to manage a happy marriage disappeared. Why did such things happen? Though the furniture and curtains of the home were exchanged for new ones, the people who lived in the house did not change. In the same way, unless we are changed, the world will not change.
>
> My dear brothers and sisters in Christ, what a joy it is to build a new church building and have worship services here! On the one hand, you may think that the church will grow automatically because we have a wonderful facility. But one thing

we must remember is that the change of facility does not guarantee the change of the church. If we want our church to be a better church, pleasing to God and being praised by people, first you and I must be changed.

Ephesians 4:22–24 says, "You were taught, with regard to your former way of life, to put off your old self, which is being corrupted by its deceitful desires; to be made new in the attitude of your minds; and to put on the new self, created to be like God in true righteousness and holiness."

Who do you think can change the world? In short, it is changed people who can change the world.

Living for the Lord until the End

In the background of the growth of Sooyoungro Church, there were countless lay people lifted up and used by the hands of God. Who are they? They were people who were changed by the Gospel. They did not just change a little, but radically. God is looking for such people and works through them. Then He makes the church grow.

The same goes for pastoral ministry. The pastor must always stand before God as a changed and renewed person. It is then that the Holy Spirit leads in the pastoral ministry. This is the essence of pastoral ministry. When the pastor tries to hold on to nonessential things, everything crumbles. God is always looking for such a pastor whose heart is always passionate for the lost soul and who considers one soul more precious than the whole world. Such a pastor is the pastor whose heart is radically changed.

It was when I was in middle school that I heard an unforgettable message from Rev. Bob Pierce when he came to Korea and spoke at a revival rally. When Rev. Pierce had been in Hong Kong and wanted to check into a hotel, there was no vacancy. It was too late to find another place to stay so he said to the clerk, "If there is an American staying alone in this hotel, would you please ask him whether I could sleep on a cot in the corner of the room?" There was a young man who willingly gave permission to share his room with Rev. Pierce. Being exhausted, Rev. Pierce fell asleep right away after he entered the room. Shortly thereafter, he awoke to the sound of weeping next to him. He was filled with compassion when he saw the man sobbing in his bed. He got up, turned on the lights, went over to the man and tried to shake him awake. While shaking him, he realized that the young man was weeping, subconsciously in his sleep and was dreaming. Rev. Pierce thought the man must have some major troubles in his life, so he woke the man, introduced himself and said to him, "I don't know what's going on, but if there is anything I can do, I'd like to help."

The awakened man was a missionary to Nepal. He had served the missionary work in Nepal for many years as a translator, but he could see no fruit at all in his missionary endeavor. During his work in Nepal, the missionary had gotten married to an American woman, and together they had a daughter. However, his daughter contracted leprosy while she was playing with dirt in the streets. The man had just dropped his daughter off at a hospital in Hawaii and was on his way back to Nepal.

How hard it must have been for that father! Years of his missionary work had brought no fruit, and his daughter contracted a miserable disease, forcing their family to be separated. It must have been very disappointing and sad for the missionary.

That evening before he went to bed, the missionary had made a decision: "How can I continue the missionary work? No fruits, my daughter with leprosy . . . when I go to Nepal, I will pack up and return to America with my wife."

However, the young man said that the Lord appeared to him in his dream that night and pleaded with him:

"If even you quit, who will bring the Gospel to the souls of Nepal? If you, too, quit ..."

The Lord's plea moved him greatly. He thought he was useless in missions because he had led no one to Christ. He thought he was just wasting mission funds. But that very night, he realized that was not how the Lord evaluated him and his missionary work. Because God had a divine plan for the souls in Nepal, the Lord was holding him! He realized that God's thoughts are different from our thoughts, and the dimension of the Gospel ministry is much higher than the human dimension. When he realized this, his heart was deeply moved, and he cried out. He could not help but cry before the sincere love and tenacity of the Lord for lost souls. Though it was a dream, the missionary was probably overjoyed because he clearly discovered the Lord's heart for lost souls.

Upon hearing the story of Pastor Bob Pierce, I felt that my life philosophy of ministry was built, despite my young age at the time.

"Yes! Whether there are converts or not, whether the church grows or not, it is completely the ministry of the Holy Spirit. If there are many of God's elected people around the church, then there must be many believers; if not, there must be fewer believers. It is something only God knows. What is important to us is to preach the Gospel to the lost soul. Preaching the Gospel itself is worth receiving the reward from God, and God considers the Gospel as the most valuable thing. It is the Holy Spirit that leads people to salvation."

Indeed, our job is merely, "How much we obey and how we obey." What the Lord values highly is our active participation in His work according to the mission of the calling. What the Lord values most highly is to live for Him with all our heart, not burying our gifts, talents, power, and time in the ground but rather using them for our Lord. What does it mean to bury them in the ground? It means that we do not do the Lord's work, using an excuse of inadequacy even though we are called. If God gave me two talents, it is okay to make two more talents. Some people need to make five more talents because they received five talents. But I need to make only two more talents because I received two talents due to my inadequacy. The Lord watches it.

It is right, therefore, to glorify God through the heart to give all if it is for the Lord, not through results of the ministry. It is the heart of the changed and renewed person to whom God promises to give the best.

"Truly I tell you," Jesus replied, "no one who has left home or brothers or sisters or mother or father or children or fields for me and the Gospel will fail to receive a hundred times as much in this present age: homes, brothers, sisters, mothers, children and fields—along with persecutions—and in the age to come eternal life" (Mark 10:29–30).

Who are the promised ones to receive the greatest awards from the Lord? They are the ones who lived for the Lord and the Gospel! The Lord promises great blessings to those who have lived for and are committed to the Gospel. If my parents, children, or wife

21

suffer in any way for the sake of the Gospel, God promises to give back a hundred times in blessings.

I openly encouraged my colleagues in pastoral ministry to live with the conviction of this important promise
of Jesus. "For what are you doing pastoral ministry?" If
we have a clear answer to this question, then there is no
reason that our ministry will be shaken. If we do pastoral
ministry not for ourselves but for the Lord, it is alright
even if we are persecuted, live in a shabby house, and
get sick. Eventually, we will have the ultimate victory
because the Lord holds the handles of the ministry.

"To the one who is victorious and does my will to the
end, I will give authority over the nations—that one 'will
rule them with an iron scepter and will dash them to
pieces like pottery'—just as I have received authority
from my Father" (Revelations 2:26–27).

No matter how severe the persecution, no matter
how difficult, no matter how painful, the Lord will give
the authority and power to rule over the nations who
keep the work of the Lord until the end, just as He gives
the authority and power to dash the pottery with an iron
scepter. What an amazing promise of God!

Doing the Lord's work is such a surprising and
impressive work. It cannot be done without joy and alle-
giance. In many verses of the Bible, there are detailed
expressions about those who are doing the work of the
Lord. The ones who do the work of the Lord are the
blessed ones. "Therefore, my brothers and sisters, you
whom I love and long for, my joy and crown, stand firm
in the Lord in this way, dear friends!" (Philippians 4:1)

Paul the apostle calls each and every believer in
the church of Philippi as "my joy and my crown." What
a happy expression! In pastoral ministry, we should at
least be able to call each and every sheep as "my joy
and my crown." If you are a shepherd, a real shepherd,

you will naturally have that kind of heart toward the sheep. This is the heart of the changed, new person who is always ready to take care of and sacrifice for the sheep. Why? It is because the shepherd has a divine calling.

God Gives Calling to Everyone

After losing my father at an early age, I was raised to become a reliable son under a kind and warmhearted mother. But our household was continuously running a downward slope in our financial situation. We lived in a neighborhood where people made tiny shacks to live in, and our house was the worst and smallest house in the neighborhood. We were always under great financial pressure. For some reason, there were always many relatives staying at our house, despite the fact that we had no father to support us. We were always lacking food, and on top of that, we could not stop the snowball effect of our debt. Out of frustration, my mother would sometimes call shamans to perform an exorcism around the house. As you can see, my family was spiritually weak and wicked. In both a worldly and spiritual way, my family had nothing to boast about.

In that situation, I tried to help my family by delivering newspapers and selling ice cream, but there was no sign of financial improvement. In fact, it was getting worse. We did not have money for food, so it was a routine that we did not have the money to pay the little tuition due to the public schools. It is fair to say that every day was like walking on thin ice because of the financial difficulties. I was called in front of the class for not paying the tuition on time, but thankfully, I was never sent home like others to bring the tuition from home. Teachers who knew my situation would specially

23

overlook my tuition, or I was benefited with an exemption. A special blessing was upon me throughout my school days.

When I started the sixth grade, a life-changing event occurred to me. The incident started when a friend named Bum-Ho Lee (an elder at Changshin Church in Seoul, Korea) transferred to my school from Kangwon Province. Being an elected class leader at the time, it was my job to sit in the back and yell out, "Attention, Bow!" to my classmates so they would say hello to the teachers. When the new student, Bum-Ho Lee, transferred to our class, the seat next to me was empty, so he was assigned to sit by me.

He started his evangelism with me immediately, but it didn't raise any negative feelings in my heart for some reason. Strangely, I thought to myself that I actually wanted to go visit the church. After several invitations, I went to church for the very first time, and that church was Changshin Church in Seoul.

My life turned completely around after I started attending Changshin Church. Could it be the evidence that God had chosen me and called me before the creation of the world? Right from the moment I stepped into the church for the first time, I couldn't help but to be filled with joy. Worship services, singing hymns, and praying made me happy. Like a fish in water, from the moment I set my feet in church, I was dancing with joy. Come to think of it, in retrospect, I was receiving God's planned, abundant grace every hour. Like a sponge absorbs water, I believed the Gospel, accepted it fully, understood it, and was delighted. Really, it was just the grace of grace. It was not because I tried to accept the Gospel, but I was able to accept the Gospel from God pouring out His grace upon me. In a sense, grace is such a 'passive form.' When God opened my heart to pour out His grace, all I had to do was simply open my heart and receive His blessings. It was solely from God's grace that a sixth grade student, only a child, nodded at the scripture, experienced God's warmth while praying, and was overjoyed in praise. As a result, the color of my face changed. From that time, school teachers would not just pass by me in the hallway but would say, "How can anyone be . . ." and pat me on the head at least once.

Even though I was only thirteen years old at that time, I was living and experiencing a mysterious feeling in God's grace. It was okay for me to live in a shack, without a father, with or without food. There were no worries that I would not be able to pay my tuition. I thought it was okay even if I died. I had no fear of death because I was confident that I would go to heaven. God's grace is a great thing. Fullness in grace led my body and mind, and because of this fullness in grace, my body and mind shined.

At that time, I experienced the fact that when I believed in Jesus more, I was able to study better. Maybe the worldly thoughts in my head vanished because my head cleared up, and I was able to concentrate like never before. I was a decent student and always did fairly well in my studies, but with God's grace, I started to stand out among others. When I did not make any mistakes, I would have perfect scores in all the sub-jects. Therefore, I was able to help my classmates when teachers were not present, explaining the main points.

Whenever I had the chance to sing in front of my class, I always sang hymns. I sang Korean hymns 318 and 186 the most.

> Softly and tenderly Jesus is calling, Calling for you and for me;

See, on the portals He's waiting and watching,
Watching for you and for me.
Come home, come home, You who are weary,
come home;
Earnestly, tenderly, Jesus is calling, Calling, O
sinner, come home! (Hymn 318)

I hear Thy welcome voice That calls me, Lord,
to Thee,
For cleansing in Thy precious blood That flowed
on Calvary.
I am coming, Lord; Coming now to Thee!
Wash me, cleanse me, in the blood That flowed
on Calvary! (Hymn 186)

Singing the fourth verse of these hymns, I wished
from the bottom of my heart that my classmates would
hear the Lord's voice to "Come Back." My friends from
that point onward addressed me as Pastor Joung.

What Should I Do to Please Jesus the Most?

It was through the influence of one of my friend's
eldest brothers that allowed me to know the Lord at
my early age. My friend's older brother (Elder Moon-Ho
Lee), whom I met right after I started going to church,
was the most respected person to me besides Jesus.
At the time, he was a clever and reliable young man
who attended Seoul National University. He was more
faithful and passionate about serving the Lord than
anyone; he was a perfect example of a Christian in my
eyes. Seeing him pray and read the Bible day and night
carved in my young soul the image of how one should
believe in and love Jesus. In my eyes, he seemed more
exemplary than any pastor. His character and way of

living were more than enough to make him my role model. He was never conceited, nor was he arrogant for attending Seoul National University. Always longing for the grace of the Lord, he attended every revival rally, and he did his best at any task given to him at church. Because of this, he was praised by everyone. Probably, my friend and I realized how we should live in faith by watching him. Back then, all the sixth grade students were busy studying for the entrance exam for junior high school. However, my friend and I were busy attending revival services here and there with his brother.

One time, we attended a revival service held by the Han River in Seoul. After receiving so much grace, we prayed all night long. The weather was so cold that the river was frozen. As we were praying, sitting on a sack on the ground in our tent, my body shivered like an aspen leaf. Under these severe conditions, my young spirit was burning with grace, and I broke down in tears, praying for God's forgiveness for my sins. The cold weather was not a problem when the forgiving Spirit of God visited me. Without knowing how much time passed by, I repented of my sins again and again. How bright and dazzling the early morning was after I prayed all that night for my sins. I was able to feel the Holy Spirit in me, fully in both body and heart. I was experiencing how the Lord's precious blood cleanses my sins away.

So I truly believe that the Holy Spirit comes and renews even the young people's hearts. One thing that cannot be done without the Holy Spirit is repentance.

"Therefore, I urge you, brothers, in view
of God's mercy, to offer your bodies as a
living sacrifice, holy and pleasing to God—
this is your true and proper worship. Do

27

not conform to the pattern of this world, but be transformed by the renewing of your mind. Then you will be able to test and approve what God's will is—his good, pleasing and perfect will" (Romans 12:1–2).

Having been cleansed of my sins and the Holy Spirit pouring abundant joy in me, the biggest change in me was my thought process. The thought of seeing Jesus in heaven dominated me even when I was sleeping or awakening, and sitting or standing. What should I do to please Jesus the most became my main concern.

Just as teachers are pleased to see students listen and study well, I wanted to feel Jesus' hands patting my head, saying, "You did well. I'm proud of you." At that time, I was living with joy, imagining how happy I would be if Jesus were smiling at me. I wanted to give myself to Jesus fully. Then the answer came naturally.

Jesus Broadens Our Dreams

Evangelism! I was confident that if I evangelized my fellow classmates, Jesus would be most pleased with me. It was Jesus who came to this world and died on the cross to save me. How pleasing it would be to Jesus if I could bring my friends to the Lord and see them saved! From then on, I started to share the Gospel with my classmates starting from the first row. There was always one goal engraved in my mind: have all my classmates believe in Jesus.

No one asked me to, but I prayed as soon as I arrived at school and before lunch, and whenever I was singing, I was always singing hymns. With these changes, my friends made fun of me at first and sometimes hid my lunch to bully me. But soon, they accepted my behavior because I was the class leader, in a position to lead them in their studies since I excelled in academics with the wisdom God had blessed me with. It was almost as if they were being absorbed into my leadership. I believe it happened because I was helping my sixth grade classmates for the entrance exam studies on behalf of the teachers. Before long, the fruits of my evangelism appeared. Bringing new friends to church became a new joy for me every weekend. I cannot describe in words how much I was deeply impressed whenever I brought new friends to church. I felt like Jesus was patting my head every time I brought my friends to church. Starting to share the Gospel with my friends, my dream was gradually growing bigger.

"I will make all the people of this country believe in Jesus."

In fact, my dream was wrong in the strict sense of the word. First of all, evangelism is not possible by a person's own power or ability. Second, whether I evangelize to people or not, if a person is chosen by God, sooner or later the person will come to God by the Holy Spirit. The absolute authority of saving souls is in God's hands.

Nonetheless, God was pleased to save people through such foolishness. Therefore, it must be clear that I dreamed such a dream because it was from God.

"For since in the wisdom of God the world through its wisdom did not know him, God was pleased through the foolishness of what was preached to save those who believe" (1 Corinthians 1:21).

Why was God pleased for His people to be saved through such foolishness of evangelism? Whatever we do to preach the Word of God, the crucifixion of Jesus would be foolish to people of the world. "For the

29

message of the cross is foolishness to those who are perishing" (1 Corinthians 1:18).

This passage means that the cross of Jesus will sound foolish to the people of the world. Only when the Holy Spirit is working in one's heart, it appears clearly that "to us who are being saved, it is the power of God" (1 Corinthians 1:18). Hence, to share the Gospel or not, the ministry of salvation is the work of God, the Trinity, but God chooses his workers to share the Gospel and bear fruits of the Gospel. Why does He do it in this way?

We can find the answers in many passages in the Bible. God does His work, but He always finds and raises his workers, trains and blesses them, and at the same time, He is pleased to be glorified by them. He can do all things directly without men's help, but He wants to raise people and to bless the people. Therefore, by giving us a passion for evangelism, it could be said that it is for our own sake. To bless and reward us, God gives us the elect in our hands.

Then what kind of person does God call to do His work and bless?

> "Brothers and sisters, think of what you were when you were called. Not many of you were wise by human standards; not many were influential; not many were of noble birth. But God chose the foolish things of the world to shame the wise; God chose the weak things of the world to shame the strong. God chose the lowly things of this world and the despised things—and the things that are not—to nullify the things that are, so that no one may boast before him" (1 Corinthians 1:26–29).

When God calls His workers, He does not choose them based on worldly standards. As for power, intellect, authority, and the family one is born into, God calls those who do not meet worldly standards and demonstrates how all is done by Him. Worldly knowledge is considered nothing before God. No one, therefore, can say that a church is revived by his or her own ability. We cannot say that we have done many of God's works because we are excellent in our ability.

This is true especially regarding our salvation. As for God's absolute authority, God never compromises. This is the same as the event of the exodus from Egypt. When God parted the Red Sea, it may have seemed that Moses divided the water with the staff; the Bible, however, clearly testifies that it was God who parted the Red Sea, not the staff. It looked like Moses did everything, but it was only possible because God had given Moses the staff in his hands. Eventually, God did everything, and Moses simply obeyed God's commands.

To save souls is God's work, and His workers are simply used for His work. God continuously seeks His workers to be used for His work. Look at what God did when He came to Moses. Moses was not the man who was not able to do God's work. He was not in the situation to say that he would be able to take the Israelites from Egypt to Canaan. How much would he be disappointed by the repetitive daily routine of taking the sheep and goats to the field in the morning and bringing them back at night for forty years? By the time he reached eighty years old, he probably had given up the old customs and memories of his social status in Egypt. He may have given up hopes and visions for his life. He was only an unknown shepherd with no special power or skill to be seen, but God called Moses just at that moment. The promise to the Israelites of finally escaping out of Egypt and leading them into Canaan was the covenant of God that had been accomplished from the time of Abraham. God's promise, therefore, must come true through whomever He chooses because it was God's plan as well as His promise. If God is doing it, it must be accomplished.

But the problem is through whom the works are done. To accomplish this great work, God assigned the task to Moses who lived in the back woods. God called Moses, gave him the vision, and was accomplishing His promise. From that moment on, Moses was not the same Moses from the past. He became a totally different Moses.

Look at when God came to Gideon. Gideon had neither the power nor the background to save the Israelites in the first place, but God came to him and called upon him by saying, "Great Warrior of Israel!"

When Jesus came to Peter, He gave the vision to Peter first. Jesus asked, "Do you love me more than these people?" And as He heard Peter's answer three times, "You know that I love you," Jesus asked Peter earnestly to "feed My sheep and raise My sheep." Peter never thought that he could be at God's service as an apostle, even after he had met the resurrected Lord. The Lord came to Peter and called upon him.

Thus, God's calling is amazing. When we receive God's call, the faith and confidence that God will lead arises. Therefore, if the calling is clear, there is no fear because when God gives a calling, it means that His plan is to be accomplished; therefore, the faith that God accomplishes always follows every work to be done.

"Do not work for food that spoils, but for food that endures to eternal life" (John 6:27).

Food that endures to eternal life! In other words, the way to live for the Gospel is the *calling*, which I received when I was in sixth grade.

Faith to Save the Family

After the call, God blessed me even more and allowed the root of my faith to be stronger. To make that possible, I believe my living with nonbelievers and in poor surroundings played a great role. Believers stand firmer and stronger when they are faced with oppression! Thankfully, God led me to stand with a stronger faith to overcome all the difficulty and oppression.

At that time, my younger sister and I were the only believers in my family. Also, we were the only believers among our relatives—we were thorns in our relatives' eyes. Since my father had passed away when I was young, distant relatives often acted and instructed me as if they were my father. One day, with fearsome eyes, one of the relatives sat me in a corner of our room and started to threaten me with a dreadful look.

"You bastard! Do you have any idea that our family is being destroyed because of you?"

The ignorant people who worshiped idols strongly believed if someone believes in Jesus, the ghost of Jesus would come into the house and destroy the family. They do not think that their sins are destroying the family, but rather they accuse the believers as the cause of every problem. For him it was not enough, so he threatened me even more.

"If you are going to continue to believe in Jesus, get out of this house! Right now!"

He got tired of threatening, so he picked up a heavy ironing board and tried to hit me with it.

"You bastard, do you want to die? Are you still going to believe in Jesus?"

A distinctive feature of Christians when they are oppressed is boldness. It does not matter who threatens and oppresses. Christian hearts will not be shaken if they have boldness given by the Holy Spirit.

"Surely, is he going to kill me? Even if he kills me, I would rather die than deny Jesus. Even if I die, it is better to be nestled in Jesus' arms, so I cannot deny Jesus!"

That was my true heart. Therefore, his threats did not move me or even cause me to blink. From that time forward, my uncle did not threaten me anymore. He probably couldn't. I had overcome one ordeal, but more persecution was yet to come.

The persecution came when my grandfather passed away. All the relatives mourned for him because he was the head of the family, and they bowed to him at the funeral. However, I could not bow to him, and I did not bow because I knew that to bow to the dead is no different from idol worship. I must have looked like a disrespectful and impertinent grandson to my relatives, so everyone started to curse me.

But I was able to endure such challenges fully. Remembering that Jesus had died on the cross for me, I didn't want to be a child who could not tolerate this much for him. I tried so hard not to be weak. Just then, words from my grandmother who loved and cared for me so much pierced my heart.

"You probably won't bow to me either when I die."

The fact that her grandson was not bowing to his grandfather saddened her more than the death of her husband. If my grandmother could know the Lord, how much she could be changed! Once this idea came into my heart, my heart was filled with hope for her to believe

34

in Jesus as soon as possible. I asked my grandmother, not trying to lose dignity.

"Grandmother, would the dead know when I bow to him?"

She raged in anger with this unexpected question. She was uncomfortable because of my attitude, but most likely, she was distressed more because of my unexpected question.

"How can the dead know?" was my grandmother's answer.

"That's exactly why I will not bow. If grandfather were alive, I would bow ten times, no, even one hundred times a day. With the same reason, I would not bow even after grandmother dies. If you are upset by that, I will bow to you diligently in advance while you are still alive."

As I said those words, I bowed to her at that moment without hesitation, and from that day on, before I went to school, I went to her room and bowed to her every day, saying, "Grandma! Receive my bow in advance!" Several months had passed with my bowing to my grandmother every morning before I went to school. One day, I do not know whether she was moved by the Spirit or not, but she said the following:

"You can stop now. I will also believe in Jesus."

Since my childhood, my grandmother loved me in a special way, and I respected her with all my heart. But after that incident, I truly tried to do my best to serve her. I went to her room and massaged her arms and legs whenever I had time. If I were to get a piece of candy, I saved it and gave it to her when I got home from school. On top of that, I tried to treat her with as much affection as possible.

"Close your eyes and open your mouth, say 'Ah!' Grandmother!"

What her grandson was doing for her was pleasing to her. Finally, she went to church with me, hand in hand, and afterwards she believed in Jesus as her Savior and Lord and went to heaven peacefully. God had answered my earnest hope.

My mother went to church as well as a result of my evangelism. I believe it was when I was in the eighth grade. I had tried to take her to church every Sunday, but it was not working well. So, as always, the biggest prayer for me was the evangelism of mom.

One day after student worship, I came home with my friends and asked her sincerely to come to church.

"Mom, come to church with me!" When I said those words, my mother started to scold me with anger out of nowhere. "*Mudang*[3] told me that all those bad things that happened to our family are because you believe in Jesus! Our family is going down because of you! If you are going to continue to believe in Jesus, get out of this house. Just get out!"

Until that day, I was hardly ever scolded by my mother. But being scolded by my mother because I believed in Jesus made me break down in tears. As I burst in tears, I told her.

"The old saying says that people grant their dead son's wish. Why won't you make your good son's wish come true? Have I ever done anything to hurt you? It was always you who hurt my heart, Mom."

I don't know why I was so sad and distressed. I cried my heart out to her. Seeing me act like this for the first time, my mother's voice softened and she said, "Alright! I will go to church, okay?"

That was the first day I worshiped God with my mother. After that incident, all of my family members

[3]   *Mudang* is a Korean version of *Shaman*.

and relatives came to church one by one and became believers in Christ.

Three Promises to God—Prayer, Worship, the Words

During the time when our only hope was to become successful to get out of poverty, God helped me understand that living for His kingdom was the biggest pleasure and joy.

"I will praise the LORD, who counsels me; even at night my heart instructs me. I keep my eyes always on the Lord. With him at my right hand, I will not be shaken" (Psalms 16:7–8).

Once I had a taste of such joy, I wanted to become a pastor who would evangelize the entire people in my nation rather than be a well-paid judge or public prosecutor. Even though at the time I was the only believer in my family, and no one recommended that I become a pastor, my heart was set with a burning flame to be a pastor. The passion for saving the lost never left me.

"I will become a pastor and have everyone in Korea believe in Jesus."

I decided that if I was going to be a pastor, I wanted to be an outstanding pastor. I didn't know exactly what it took to be a great pastor, but I wanted to be the kind of pastor that God would pat on the head as a sign of His approval. It definitely was not a selfish desire for worldly success. I just wanted to be a good pastor who would be approved and admired by Jesus. I wanted to please Jesus' heart. As soon as I received God's calling in this way when I was only a sixth grader, I began to construct my lifelong plans.

"I'm going to become a pastor who will be praised by God. To do so, if I can go to school, I will go to

Kyunggi Junior High School, Kyunggi High school, and Seoul National University,[4] and then go to a seminary to become an ordained pastor."

At the time, Kyunggi Junior High and Kyunggi High Schools were schools for elite students from rich and distinguished families. No matter how excellent I was academically, I could not even dream of making it to these schools because of my family's financial situation. However, thinking that if God allowed me, there was no place I would not be able to go, I set my goal on Kyunggi Junior High School and started studying very hard. It wasn't for selfish desires to have a mark of the elite course. If I was going to do God's work, I wanted to study at the most difficult and top schools, and then I wanted to evangelize to the people in the world. Anyway, I thought God would be more pleased if I studied hard and received excellent grades.

Probably, God might have accepted my heart. Out of four boys' classes in our school, only six students were accepted to Kyunggi Junior High School, and five out of these six were from my class. It is to that extent that our class studied with me, the leader of the class, and were faithful in Christian life as well. Many of my friends whom I helped to come to Jesus at that time, have become well-respected elders today.

After starting junior high school, God took a new grip on my heart to fulfill his calling. With determination, God led me to pursue deeper levels of faith beginning very early from elementary school through impressionable times in my youth. At that time after I went to junior high school, I was faced with certain crises. In

---

4   At that time, Kyunggi Junior High School and Kyunggi High School were the best junior and high schools in Korea. Seoul National University is still considered to be the best university in Korea.

one circumstance, dating pretty girls who were attractive to the boys, I felt that I was in a crisis of losing the grace I received in elementary school. Remembering how joyful it was to live in and be with Jesus, I had to pray so that the precious grace of the Lord would not leave me.

"Jesus, what should I do to hold the grace I have received from you? How can I live godly?"

While I was praying for this request, the Holy Spirit gave me the wisdom to make three decisions. The first decision was to come to church three times a day and pray. I went to church on the way to school, after school, and after dinner for prayer.

After I had made up my mind, I never skipped going to church three times a day. Sometimes I not only prayed three times a day, but also I prayed through the night. I prayed while I was walking, before I went to bed, and even while I was playing with my friends. Because the Holy Spirit was holding me, He led me to pray even more under the financial difficulties of my family.

One day, my sister cried her way to school because she had no money for her Parent-Teacher Association (P.T.A.) fee. As her older brother, seeing her cry hurt my heart so much that it was on my mind all day long. In those days, I couldn't help but pray for the matter all day long. I prayed hard about it at church on my way to school, and I continued to pray as I walked around the schoolyard. I could not stop praying.

"God, it is time for you to provide. It is time for you to provide."

The amazing thing was that whenever I prayed like that, God quickly answered my prayer. When I arrived home, someone was waiting for me to make a donation for my tuition. He was an angel sent by God. With that money, we were able to take care of my sister's P.T.A. fee.

Not only did God answer my prayers promptly, but my experiences with God through prayer were growing deeper and deeper also. Perhaps it is because my prayers were not pushed by men but led by the Holy Spirit. The grace that comes from the Holy Spirit every hour was way beyond my imagination. At that time, I was able to experience through my body, my heart, and my spirit what the presence of the Holy Spirit was and how to be confident of His presence. Because of the indescribably strong moving of the Holy Spirit, on some nights, I would pray all night long.

Although the disciples followed Jesus for three years and called Him, "Christ, the Son of the living God," and it is clear that they were born again, they were not yet baptized by the Holy Spirit at that point. After Acts 2:1, we can realize that they were baptized by the Spirit for the first time.

"When the day of Pentecost came, they were all together in one place. Suddenly a sound like the blowing of a violent wind came from heaven and filled the whole house where they were sitting. They saw what seemed to be tongues of fire that separated and came to rest on each of them. All of them were filled with the Holy Spirit and began to speak in other tongues as the Spirit enabled them" (Acts 2:1–4).

As it is clearly stated in the Bible, when the Holy Spirit is present, one can see, hear, and feel Him. I clearly understood what Acts chapter 2 meant. Especially when I prayed all night repenting for my sins and for my uncomfortable heart to be moved clearly, the Holy Spirit was present powerfully. Around one or two in the morning, when all my strength had been consumed due to my prayers, the Holy Spirit became present and wrapped around me with burning energy like tongues of fire. No one had taught me about the Holy Spirit's appearance or what the gift of the Holy Spirit was, but the Holy Spirit Himself came in a special way to me. On days like that, I had unusual experiences and stayed up all night. Because of those special experiences, sometimes I went to church after dinner, stayed up all night praying, and then I went to school the next morning. I couldn't help but fall asleep at school on such days.

I was filled with heavenly joy by experiencing God's powerful grace. Whenever I went home, the financial pressure pressed down on our family; however, whenever I prayed at church, the eternal joy filled with His goodness embraced my soul. God was responding to my first decision to keep my faith.

My second decision was not to miss the church's official worship service, no matter what happened and despite any conditions. As for that decision, I don't recall ever missing the church's official worship service throughout junior high, high school, and even throughout college.

My third decision was to read at least one chapter of the Bible every day. Following this decision, from the first year in junior high school, I was able to read the whole Bible several times in a year.

Looking back, I realize that the reason I was able to decide and carry out my three decisions was because of God's grace to strengthen my faith firmly like a rock after I received His call. As there was no family member for me to be spiritually accountable to, God poured out his abounding grace on me to let my faith grow.

Because of these three decisions, no matter how much I have sinned and been shaken and tempted by Satan, I have stood right back up every time and was able to overcome the six years of junior high and high school in spiritual victory. Also, the spiritual experiences from the three decisions showed clearly that the call from the Lord was not an emotional and temporary decision of a child. God was strengthening the foundation of my faith by letting me experience clearly and lively the fact that God is living, God is always with me, and the Holy Spirit controls everything in history through prayer, the scripture, and the worship services.

God Ties Us Down Because He Loves

When I was attending Seoul National University after I graduated from junior high and high school, I had only one wish: "When can I work 24 hours only for God?" So even in my busy schedule, I volunteered to photocopy the Sunday bulletin for a church with over 500 in attendance. The work for the Lord that started when I was in junior high School was always a joy. Only the ones who have served for the Lord could understand how great and overwhelming the joy is when we give our royalty and services for the Lord.

During that time, I was going through a difficult period. When I was young, my family struggled financially—even more as the years passed by. We were not living in a good house, but besides a shack, we still had a tile-roofed house, so our living conditions were not so impoverished. However, we had many relatives asking for financial help, and since my mother's character was not very suitable for working, we had to live with more debt every day. My gentle but inflexible mother was responsible for the exponential progression of our debts every year.

At that time, borrowing money from neighbors meant having to pay great interest. If my mother had begged the neighbor from whom we borrowed money to delay the deadline, she might have made it easier for our family. But she paid them back with money she borrowed from another neighbor and so on. So our debt doubled and tripled. 10,000 won soon became 100,000 won, and 100,000 won soon became 1,000,000 won. The house we lived in was soon gone, and we had to settle in a shabby shack. However, even that shack was torn down sometime later.

My family literally had no place to go and to sleep. Nonetheless, insurmountable debt pressed our shoulders. While I was attending Seoul National University and my sister was attending Kyunggi Girl's High School, our family became ruined totally. We had to rent on monthly payments a one-room facility barely large enough to sleep in.

In desperation, my mother would try to make a living by going around the neighborhood and holding up a rubber basin with vegetables for sale. But when she returned home, the vegetables were in the basin. My mother was so shy, introverted, and gentle that she could not yell out, "Vegetables for sale!" Watching her repeat this process day after day, I told her to stop what she was doing.

"Mother, please stop working! I will find some way!"

From that day on, I took on all the financial responsibilities. Even in the midst of all of these struggles, God sent me His angels and graciously let me continue my studies. Miraculous hands helped me and followed me every step of the way. However, I was still left to take care of my sister's tuition, my books, living costs of our family, debt payment, and our family's rent.

I had no time to take a rest from tutoring kids during my four years in college. Being a resident tutor, I had several tutoring sessions, so I faced time and physical limitations. School studies were done in the library with concentration only when classes were canceled, so taking some time off to study for myself was only possible in my dreams. All through college, my health was put to the test. Even though I had a healthy physique, four years without much sleep caused me to become nothing but skin and bones. This routine continued for four long years. I couldn't imagine enjoying the romance of college even for a moment. My college years flew by as I spent most of my time tutoring high school students for their national college entrance examinations. In the middle of all this, the only joy I had was attending church worship services every Sunday with the students I was tutoring. I had my hands full serving all day, but that one day was the only day I was able to feel freedom. To stay in God's house was rest and joy for me.

"Better is one day in your courts than a thousand elsewhere; I would rather be a doorkeeper in the house of my God than dwell in the tents of the wicked" (Psalms 84:10).

It was through the power of prayer that I was able to withstand the extreme financial pressures and hardships at that time. I prayed three times a day at any price and used to sing hymns on the way to school, back home from school, and off to tutoring work. When I walked, it was time to praise, and whenever I had a moment to be alone or to sit down for a minute, it was time for me to pray. In the midst of prayer and praise, God touched my exhausted body and heart. He protected me from suffering and worry from the complicated matters and prevented me from putting my thoughts on unnecessary things. God gave me strength to live each day faithfully so that I was able to keep my mind and thoughts.

After the graduation ceremony, as I knelt down to pray at the church, tears rolled down from my eyes because I felt that graduating itself was such a miracle for me. Even though I attended a prestigious school that many people could only imagine attending, four years at the university had no romance at all, nor was I able to study to the fullest. Whenever I recalled how I finished my studies, it was just incredible. A part of me was overwhelmed with deep gratitude, and a part of me was sad. So these words just burst out of my mouth: "Lord, what in the world is this? I studied so hard to come to this university, but I wasted all four years only tutoring instead of studying. Why did I have to spend my time like this?"

All of a sudden, I was very distressed, and a deep sigh came out. Maybe God was not able to tolerate such complaints. He spoke to me clearly.[5]

"If I had not tied you up, do you really think that you could be my servant?"

It was clearly the Lord's voice. The Lord said that the busy and hard times were all in God's divine plan and providence. Why? According to Him, if He had not done so, I could have backed out of His call. If God had not tied me down for my four years of college, truly I could have taken another road instead.

After getting into Seoul National University through studying hard faithfully, I had many offers for marriage. The pastors' families, elders' families, and even a private tutoring family made continuous offers for me to be their son-in-law. There were many people around me who loved me that much. Thanks to them, I was able to get through my hard life without losing strength, but

---

[5]   In this book, when the writer mentions that "God told me" or "the Lord said to me," he does not say, "a new Prophetic Revelation" or "Insufficiency or Continuation of Special Revelation." Rather, he says, "Illumination of the Holy Spirit." Even today, the Holy Spirit who is living and working speaks, teaches, and guides God's people in His Illumination providentially, not as a Prophetic Special Revelation.

who knows what would have happened if I had gotten into a relationship with anyone or gotten married? Who knows if I could have lived a completely different life, if I had such reservations in my mind?

God did not want me to forget the calling. He tied up all my time to concentrate only on the call, and during those times, he disciplined me and clearly showed me the light of hope toward the Lord. "When will I be able to live twenty-four hours a day only for the Lord? When can I work twenty-four hours fully like a cattle only for His works?" As the busy and difficult times were getting more serious, my dream was becoming clearer. God made me wish more and more for the joy of working for eternal bread, not for rotting bread.

CHAPTER 2

Discipline: The Answer Is Found Only In God

There Is God's Intention in Discipline

If there is one thing that God allows for those who are called, it is a time of discipline. Through discipline, Christians are born again as a people who long for heaven while living on earth. God's people can realize that earthly things are momentary and hollow, but things that belong to heaven are eternal and valuable. Through discipline with money, they will understand that adherence to money and possessions is vain. Also through discipline in the flesh, they will realize that the flesh is of finite value and will soon fade away like dry grass.

Discipline on human relationship teaches us that we have only one God in whom we can put our ultimate trust and that we understand what it means to "love one another." Discipline on wealth, power, and fame teaches us that all things under the sun are momentary and that living for God is the true direction of life.

"Not only so, but we also rejoice in our sufferings, because we know that suffering produces perseverance; perseverance, character; and character, hope" (Romans 5:3–4). Discipline leads us to heavenly hope. God gives a calling of stewardship in money to those who have been disciplined with money. God also gives through intercessory prayer workers who have gone through many difficult times when they had no choice but to get down on their knees and pray.

In pastoral ministry, we go through many discipline in many ways. There is one thing that I cannot help but to confess about them. If we do not work with the Holy Spirit, it is absolutely impossible to succeed in pastoral ministry. Without being anointed by the Holy Spirit, without being together with the Holy Spirit, and without engagement of the Holy Spirit, the pastoral ministry cannot succeed. On one occasion, Jesus gave his disciples this command:

"Do not leave Jerusalem, but wait for the gift my Father promised, which you have heard me speak about" (Acts 1:4).

The Lord Christ told his disciples to be baptized by the Holy Spirit first because he knew His disciples could never have victory in the world without the Holy Spirit.

I have learned one thing through the discipline I experienced from childhood until now: *waiting*. Reflecting back on my life, I even think that God allowed all the suffering and discipline in my life just to teach me to wait. When I wait for the promised Spirit of the Lord, the Holy Spirit comes and solves all the problems one by one. But when I am impatient and try to deal with the difficulties with my own resources, I always fail. We all have to wait. The process of waiting for the promised baptism of the Holy Spirit is the meaning of discipline.

When we pastors try to overcome the difficulties in pastoral ministry with our own strength, it will eventually hurt not only us but the sheep given to us. Nonetheless, the reason we do not wait for the time of the Holy Spirit's work is because we have not tasted and experienced yet the beauty of doing ministry through the Holy Spirit. The disciples of Jesus followed Him for three years and witnessed and experienced many wonders, signs, and miracles. However, they failed in the ministry of salvation until the Holy Spirit of the Lord came to them. If they failed, then we must have failed one hundred percent. Why? Because the ministry of saving the souls, changing the souls, and bringing up the souls belongs only to the work of the Holy Spirit. Without the work of the Holy Spirit, there will be no fruit. That is the pastoral ministry. A pastor, therefore, must be a tool of the Holy Spirit. When the Holy Spirit fills us with His fullness, we see evidences of the work of the Holy Spirit in our lives and ministries.

We Live Not for Death but for God

Growing up I had been through a lot of unsolvable problems and suffering for which I desperately sought God's help in prayer. What was it that God wanted from me in those times of discipline?

"Only God!" That was it. God made me continuously realize that He has the key for all problems. God taught me that no matter how desperate the situation is and no matter how difficult the problem is, it could be turned around immediately when God intervened. Therefore, He made me realize that the key to the solution of all problems eventually is only in the Lord's hands. Through these times of discipline, God gave me the habit of just waiting on Him thirstily. God made me pray again and again.

"Lord, now it's time for you to solve the problems!"

Reflecting on the past, I now realize the reason why I took up the financial burdens of my family, just as the actual head of my family, was because God wanted to teach me the habit of waiting on Him. Through that habit, I have experienced the indescribable grace of God and the gifts of the Holy Spirit.

When I entered Kyunggi Junior High School, God clearly showed me that the answer is only found in Him. Although I entered the school, I could not afford the tuition. I became more anxious as the deadline drew closer and closer. When I came to a realization that there was no possible way for me to afford the school, I sat on the floor and just cried out. My mother cried with me when she saw me crying. It was a day when I painfully realized that my family could not support my studies in any way.

Several days later, my neighbor who owned a small grocery store at the opposite side of our house visited my house holding a newspaper in his hand and asked me, "Did you read the paper? Your name is in it."

It was an unbelievable thing. But there was my name in the newspaper, with an introduction saying that I graduated from Chang-Shin Elementary School and was accepted to Kyunggi Junior High School. To my surprise, I was selected as one of the recipients of a scholarship from a famous congressman named Mr. Guan-Sik Min, who was also a graduate of Kyunggi Junior High School. Every year, he selected one male and one female student to receive full tuition scholarships until their graduation. I was selected as one of the recipients that year. God was leading me in such a direction that I could never expect or imagine. I had applied for Kyunggi Junior High to please God, and He had answered my prayers in this way. I could not help but pray even more diligently. The reason I prayed seriously three times a day was because He helped me in these times and led my life in such a way.

My family situation, however, was getting worse and worse. When I entered high school, our debts increased even more. Our living situation was indescribable. But I realized later on that God disciplined me to be His servant during this special and painful period.

During this period of my life, I suffered not only by my family's situation, but I saw people in this world becoming more depraved. Even in the church, there were disputes and divisions repeatedly. Watching this situation, I gradually felt disillusioned and suffered over life in the world.

Watching over and experiencing both a difficult family situation and the corruption of the world, I realized two things: one was that if I live more in this world, I only experience pain in this world, and the other was that if I live more in this world, then I would commit sins more and more. Therefore, I drew the conclusion that it was a blessing for a believer who was saved already to leave this world as quickly as possible.

With that conclusion, I really wanted to die quickly, but I could not commit suicide because my life belonged to the Lord. "So how could I die?" I found a way to die. It was to die with fasting prayers. As soon as summer vacation started in my junior year of high school, I started to pray with fasting.

Reflecting on it now, it is a sort of funny story, but at that time, I cried out seriously to the Lord with fasting prayers. "God, please take me. I don't want to live any more. I really don't want to live any longer. Please call me and take me to you as soon as possible."

The first two days passed on just like that, but there was no answer from God. He was completely silent. I prayed desperately for God to take my life. It looked like my life was over, but I was still alive. I was starting to get very hungry. I was used to skipping meals, but the hunger that I experienced during this time was really unbearable because I stopped eating any food entirely. Anyway, I was still breathing. I was afraid that I still would not die even after forty days of fasting. My heart sank. What good is it if I don't die after fasting like this for forty days! I couldn't imagine living for forty days starving like this. I decided that dying as soon as possible was the solution. On the third day, I prayed with all my strength. I was determined to die while I was praying to God, so I called out to God as loud as I could. "Lord, please take my life as soon as possible! I don't want to live any longer. Please take me! Please take me away quickly!"

I cannot imagine how the Lord would have felt when His own child was crying out for Him to take away his life. God could not watch me crying out any longer. On the third day, He came to speak to me, and He gave me His clear voice.

"You are dead!"

It was clearly the Lord's voice.

"You are dead! So can't you live for me from now on? Can't you live for me? Can't you live for me?"

At the moment, the Lord said that I had already died. And He entreated me three times to live for Him.

"Can't you live for me?"

The voice of the Lord, asking me to live for Him instantly and completely solved the problem of death that I had in my life. The Lord taught me clearly to live, not to die, but to live for the Lord.

In that moment, I personally experienced that it is okay if I kneel down and pray when a hardship as serious as death comes to us. At that time, I vividly experienced that if God speaks just once, every issue is cleared. If your life is so miserable to the point you seek death, then wait for God with all your heart. Then the Lord will deal with the core issues with you and begin to solve all the problems.

"I have been crucified with Christ and I no longer live, but Christ lives in me. The life I now live in the body, I live by faith in the Son of God, who loved me and gave himself for me" (Galatians 2:20).

Let God Go before You

In 1969, I was preparing for Kangdosa[6] examination. There were some people who took a vacation and stayed in the library just to study for the test. However, strangely only I was focusing on working for my church instead of preparing for the examination. One of the reasons was from having constant questions in my mind.

"I will be an ordained pastor if I pass this exam. But am I really qualified to be a pastor? Is becoming a pastor the only possible way for me to live for God through my life? Isn't it possible for me to live just for Christ as a laity?"

As soon as such ideas came into my mind, I wanted to have a convincing answer from God regarding being a pastor. So I went up to Mt. Chung-gae and started praying while fasting.

"Lord, please give me just one word! Do I have to be a pastor?"

---

[6] *Kangdosa* is an individual licensed to preach until he is ordained officially as a pastor.

I started fasting prayers from Monday, and I talked frankly about my heart to God.

"Father, I think it is better for me to serve you as a laity. Do I really need to be a pastor? Lord, do you really want me to be a pastor?"

I started praying on the mountain on Monday, but there was no answer until Thursday. Moreover, it started to rain on Thursday. I had no choice but to hold up an umbrella and pray. Doing so for a while, I suddenly felt ashamed of myself holding an umbrella to avoid the rain. I was in fasting prayer to confirm my calling, but look at me holding an umbrella to avoid rain. With shameful feelings about my image, I immediately threw away the umbrella. Shortly after I started praying while kneeling on a rock in the pouring rain, I heard God's clear voice. He spoke to me to be a pastor. How can I possibly express in words the overwhelming joy of the moment!

"Hallelujah! Hallelujah! Thank you. I will be a pastor!"

On my way down from the mountain after I received the answer from the Lord, I felt like I was walking on a cloud. Ever since this incident, God had always walked ahead of me and led my pastoral ministry. He always led me with the blessing of Jehovah Jireh.[7]

Every pastor goes through a hard time. Sometimes, pastors are faced with desperate situations. However, if they pray with all their hearts before God and listen to God's answers, the problem will always soon be resolved. Also, the problem will turn into a testimony, and it becomes an incident of blessing.

"But the LORD said to me, 'Do not say, "I am only a child." You must go to everyone I send you to and say whatever I command you. Do not be afraid of them, for

---

[7]   In Hebrew "The Lord will provide."

I am with you and will rescue you,' declares the LORD" (Jeremiah 1:7–8).

Receiving God's Sign through Prayers of Tears

I was working at Sooyoungro Church by Sooyoung Rotary, and the church was continuously growing, but there was one big problem of the church not having enough parking spaces. Due to a lack of parking spaces, if church members parked their cars on both sides of the streets while they were in worship service, their cars were often towed away. Although our church members were blessed through worship service, after they realized their cars were towed away, their faces would change, about to cry. Since this was a repetitive problem every Sunday, as the pastor, I was in a heart-broken state. I thought if this issue were not solved, maybe nobody would come to Sooyoungro Church to worship. With this thought, I went down beside the pulpit and started to pray with tears to the Lord.

"Lord, please give us a parking lot. Give us a parking lot."

Thinking about the church members' hearts whose cars got towed away, I could not help crying. It seems that God gives immediate answers when pastors pray especially with tears. That night, God answered me in my dream, saying, "I will give you the parking lot."

Shortly after this, I was invited to have lunch together with the landlord's only Christian daughter. Suddenly, I felt like this was not just a coincidence, but that God made an urgent meeting to fulfill His plans. With that conviction, I announced God's promise to the whole church congregation.

"God has promised to give us the land. Do you also want our church to purchase the land? If you do, please raise both of your hands and say 'Hallelujah.'"

Everyone responded.

"Hallelujah."

The land was perfect for our church parking lot.

"Do any of the elders oppose?"

No one raised a hand.

"Okay. Let's move forward."

As soon as the conversation was over, everything developed at top speed. The elders of the church immediately met with the landowner and made a contract, even though we only had money for an initial deposit. Later, I asked them, "How could you so confidently make the contract without fear?"

They all replied with a smile. "We thought someone had already given the money to you because you said you received God's promise. Ha ha!"

I had just suggested to proceed trusting in God's promise. Before the contract, I never mentioned making offering pledges for the church parking spaces. I simply announced to the church to proceed with this project without any doubt because there was a clear sign from the Lord that He would open the door for us. Because of this, the progress of the project was very fast, and soon the time came for us to make the down payment. However, no one was stepping up to contribute the money. In this situation, I had no choice but to depend only on God in prayer. I, beside the pulpit, and my wife, under the pulpit, started fasting and praying.

"Lord, you promised that you would provide, but why do you not give to us?"

I don't remember exactly how long I prayed in that way. When I prayed on early Sunday morning, God answered me with a scripture.

"I will go before you and will level the moun-
tains; I will break down gates of bronze
and cut through bars of iron. I will give you
hidden treasures, riches stored in secret
places, so that you may know that I am
the LORD, the God of Israel, who sum-
mons you by name" (Isaiah 45:2–3).

At the moment that I received these words from God,
I shouted with joy.
"It's all done! It's all done! It's all done! Hallelujah!
Thank you!"
When God answers this way, it is already all done.
Even though I saw no evidence, when God answers this
way, it means that God has already prepared everything.
That day in my Sunday sermon, I shared this fact as
a testimony with the whole congregation. I, with conviction, proclaimed that I surely received the answer from
the Lord, and that God said He had hidden resources for
us. The whole congregation listened attentively to my
testimony and was blessed. But no money, no offering,
came in that night.
The following day was the deadline for the down
payment. If we could not pay, the contract would be
cancelled, and on top of that, we would have to pay a
penalty. I wondered how God would answer.
That afternoon, the church members who lived all
over the city of Busan, transferred their offerings into the
church account. The amount started in a small amount,
about 100,000 won (about $100 in 2014 exchange
rate), to 1,000,000 won (about $1,000 in 2014 rate),
grew bigger and bigger, and eventually became more
than we needed. Even later, the offerings continued to
come in, so much that we were able to pay off the land
within one year. I never asked the congregation to make

offering pledges even once, but God had already moved the church members' hearts to give voluntarily. I was so thankful to the Lord that the parking lot was purchased not through one particular wealthy person's offering, but through devotional giving of the entire congregation. That year, during the congregational meetings, the whole congregation stood up and danced with joy. It was because we were able to purchase the golden land as the church parking lot, and the actual annual offerings exceeded the annual budget. The annual congregational meeting became a festival, praising God and giving thanks to Him for what He had blessed.

Put Your Energy into God instead of Using It to Persuade People

I am sharing this experience for this reason. There are always many issues in pastoral ministry, whether it is related to church building projects or church growth issues. But we often face difficult situations because we change the priority to solve the problem. First of all, we must receive God's answer. When we skip this first thing, we fall into a whirlpool of problems.

Are you planning something important? Then you must receive the clear answer from the Lord first. If the answer doesn't come quickly, then you have to wait until He answers. Whether you plant a church, construct a church building, or go out in the mission field as a missionary, the most significant thing is for you to receive the answer from the Lord. If you sincerely confess that the sovereignty of the pastoral ministry belongs to God, you should not just start doing the ministry without a certain plan and process. There is nothing more arrogant than just starting God's work.

Put your energy before God instead of trying to solve and persuade through people. God is not mute. He will give you answers in certain ways. When God gives you a message, the Holy Spirit will solve all your problems, and at that time, the best solution will come out.

People who wait for God's answer will receive immeasurable courage and power. As we all know, our own boldness and nature can be shaken easily in a crisis. But if the Holy Spirit answers, even a coward becomes courageous, and the unable becomes able. When you experience this power of the Holy Spirit, your message will be alive, and your face will shine. Every word will be empowered with God's authority.

On the other hand, if you first do something in your own will, it will be seen in your countenance. When things do not go as planned, the pastor will become fretful. His message will be delivered with anxiety and fretfulness. As a result, the congregation that receives the message will also be fretful. By scolding church members, there are actually many cases that the pastor becomes the key person to cause internal troubles in the church.

I cannot do anything right when my head is overflowing with my own thoughts or when my heart is burdened by my own problems. During times like this, I need to be connected to the Lord until my thoughts are cleared. It doesn't matter whether it is dawn or in the middle of the night, I go to God and hold onto the Lord. I did this when I was a teenager in middle and high schools and when I was an intern pastor. Whenever I was pushed to the limit, I would go up to the mountain and sit on the edge of the cliff and cry out. "Lord, do as you will. I will die falling off the cliff while praying if you don't give me the answer by tonight." I thought I would have something to say in heaven if I really died while struggling in prayer since it wasn't a suicide.

In life, we are often faced with life-or-death situations. However, God never ignores His children who pray with such desperate hearts. He touches the broken hearts of those who are desperately holding on to Him. He answers their prayers. The Holy Spirit comes like fire and a dove. When He comes, it is impossible to express the joy in words.

Sometimes, God does not give an immediate answer, but He always answers those who sincerely seek Him. Sometimes, a mere determination to try to seek Him with a clear decision even to die causes God to answer your prayers at that moment. Long prayers, therefore, are not necessary as sufficient prayer. God always sees the hidden motives in our hearts and whether they are fit for Him or not. Therefore, to pray long is nothing to boast about to people.

When I was a senior in high school, my heart started to feel desperate as the college entrance examination date drew near because I knew I could not afford to go to the university. I felt I would have to give up on any account. Although I continually went to church three times a day to pray, my heavy and burdened heart did not rest in peace. For that reason, one day I went up to Mt. Sam-Gak to pray to God with a desperate heart to die. I intentionally picked a precipitous cliff and went up to the top. It was a very dangerous cliff. If I made even a small mistake, I would fall down and die. Then I stood at the edge of the cliff and started to pray with this mind: "If I die, I will die." I was on the top of the cliff in the mountain in the middle of winter, and the weather was severely cold. It was not easy to withstand the freezing, cold wind directly without any proper winter jacket. I probably would have frozen to death at that time if God had not given His grace. I believe He saved me because I had a mission that I had to accomplish. I prayed earnestly with all my might until my back was covered with sweat. When I stopped praying, the sweat on my back started to freeze, and I could not bear it any longer. I thought I prayed for a long time, but only twenty minutes had passed when I looked at my watch. How fickle are human minds! Although I climbed up that mountain with a determination to die, I climbed down the mountain because I could not overcome the cold.

However, God already had an answer. A supporter showed up to provide me with a full scholarship for four years of my college before I was even accepted anywhere.

Praying at the risk of your life means waiting solely for God's answer. It is to confess that there is no other way if God does not provide resolution. The Lord stretches out His almighty and helping arms to us when we confess with all our heart, will, and sincerity that He is the only one who has the ultimate sovereignty in our lives. Though I could not stay long on Mt. Sam-Gak, through this experience God led me to completely rest lordship of my life upon Him.

Before I became an ordained pastor, I went through several training sessions in such ways as I have already mentioned thus far. How amazing is God's absolute sovereignty toward human life! The Lord taught me time and time again that we cannot live by our strength but only by God's leading. Through the process of discipline, God taught me that the secret of victory was giving up my own strength and living with God's power. Therefore, I stopped seeking advice from people when I met some difficulty in my ministry. The Lord taught me repeatedly that the key is to kneel down before God rather than discussing the difficulty with people.

One of the reasons for failures in pastoral ministry is because pastors are more concerned about people's eyes than the Lord's eye toward them. Whenever you are concerned over criticism or slander and how people think of you, you will try to talk to people and try to change their opinion. This only causes bigger problems. When people slander or neglect you, if you will focus on "'How does the Lord look at me? What does He say?," such pastors will reap the fruits of joy.

"Cast your cares on the LORD and He will sustain you; He will never let the righteous fall" (Psalms 55:22).

If the Lord speaks to you or reveals Himself to you, there is nothing on earth to be afraid of. In such times, church members will know that you are a pastor whom God dwells in, uses, and approves. When this happens, one cannot describe the joy for the coming blessings on the pastoral ministry.

Are you going through a hardship? Get on your knees only in front of the Lord. Then the Lord will resolve and show you the way. He expects to see you through that time if you have the faith to recognize the fact that the pastoral ministry is completely done by the Holy Spirit. A pillar of clouds will soon appear. Even at that time, we have to wait longer until the pillar of clouds moves. When the pillar of clouds moves, we also move. This is the pastoral ministry.

CHAPTER 3

Preparation: God Uses As Much As We Love

God Uses the Man of Love the Most Greatly

Occasionally, I have the opportunity to have conversations with seminary students. In these meetings, I usually hear the question, "How can I prepare myself for pastoral ministry?" Many people already agree with the fact that "God uses a person as much as he is prepared," so now their concern is how to prepare.

By that time, I use the word, *love* incredibly much. Just as the greatest command of the law is love, the best preparation for a pastor is love. The essential nature of God, who created and reigns over human beings, is love. Therefore, He takes great joy to use a man of love.

Take a look at David, the son of Jesse. Jesse had eight sons, but why did he entrust the flock of sheep to David? The reason is because when lions and bears would attack the sheep, David risked his own life to save his flocks. Where did he get the courage to kill the lions and bears holding their whiskers? Because David had the faith that if God was with him, he could rescue the sheep and even be able to kill lions and bears. The faith of David is based on love. His love for the sheep at the risk of his life made David's faith as firm as a rock. Because David was such a person, Jesse was able to entrust a flock of sheep to David. Jesse did not have to worry about his flock as long as he entrusted David to take care of them.

When God is searching for His servant, He is looking for someone like David. God who values one man more than the whole world will not entrust His sheep to just anyone.

"To whom do I have to entrust my sheep to feed good grass? To whom do I have to entrust my sheep to fatten them? Who will take good care of my sheep?"

God is watching us with this heart in our pastoral ministry field.

The sovereignty of pastoral ministry belongs to God. If God entrusts many, then the church becomes big. If God entrusts little, then church remains small. But whether a church is big or small, all pastoral ministries are important because they are all the work of the Lord. The fact that God's sheep are under our care is itself a great blessing. God is searching for a person who will not allow His sheep to starve to death, although He entrusts great numbers of sheep. He is also searching for a faithful person who appreciates even a small number of sheep and faithfully takes care of the sheep. No matter what, it is totally God's grace that we, the insufficient, are able to work the pastoral ministry. God's calling to pastoral ministry itself is indescribable gratitude and impression.

Then what is our best response of the called to God's calling? It is to become a man of love. To love the sheep, the church, and the Lord is the only preparation we need. We need to become a kind of person who expands the width and depth of love. A person who is filled with love is doing the given tasks well. Take a look around. A cook who cooks with love makes the best food with all his heart. Is not the love and affection the key for cooking? If there is love, deep love, cooking for every meal is not a troublesome task. When a husband is sick, although his wife needs to prepare meals with natural healthy food for him, if there is love, she would not express her complaints. For her husband to get better, she would regard her work as nothing, since she loves her husband. If there is love, mothers will not think it is troublesome work to wake up at the break of dawn to prepare an early meal and take care of her children. Instead, she would only wish that her loved ones will receive good nutrients and be healthy from the food she prepared for them. This is the heart of a person with love. This is the reason that to love more is to work better.

Pastors who love the sheep should have this kind of heart. First, God knows well if a pastor has this kind of heart or not, and second, the sheep notice it, too. It cannot be feigned. It can be seen through our faces and through our conversations. It can be known through a sermon and when working together; it can really be shown through actions. Whether a pastor loves truly, superficially, or selfishly clearly appears even more apparent as time goes by. The sheep will know if the pastor hates them instead of loving them, or if the pastor curses them instead of blessing them.

If we raise a dog at home, we can easily see how sensitive the dog is to the love of his master. The dog follows around and wags his tail when he feels the true affection from his master, but when he feels like his master hates him, he wags his tail gently but will not follow him around. Eventually, some dogs will even take precautions against their own master.

If we are filled with deep affection toward our sheep, they have no choice but to follow the master whole heartedly. Yes, they will follow you. It is the principle of pastoral ministry.

God has used men of love greatly. Joseph did not spend his life blaming his brothers who sold him in slavery and Potiphar's wife who sent him to prison by falsely accusing him of rape. He never took revenge. Instead he helped even his brothers' descendants to have a comfortable life.

Look at Moses, a servant of God. He had to suffer a tremendous amount because of the sins of the Israelites. They often resented Moses by longing for their old lives as slaves in Egypt and sinned toward God. Watching over the repeated rebellion of His people, God said to Moses that He would completely wipe out the Israelites and build a new nation through Moses. But Moses did not reply to the Lord, "You are right, Lord. Please do as you will." Rather, he offered his life for the sake of the Israelites to deter God's mind: "So Moses went back to the Lord and said, 'Oh, what a great sin these people have committed! They have made themselves gods of gold. But now, please forgive their sin—but if not, then blot me out of the book you have written'" (Exodus 32:31–32).

Moses was a leader who loved his people. Though the Israelites were wicked, he loved them to the point that his name might be erased from the Book of Life in order to save them. The confession of Moses was not disguised or hypocritical. There is no way that God would not know it if that were the case. God must have been pleased by reading Moses' sincere heart toward the Israelites, although He was furious about the rebellion of His people. If I have to give one reason why God chose Moses, it would be his cherished love for the Israelites.

There are many people around the world who have power and are highly intellectual, but it is hard to find a person with great love. God is still searching for that one person who has a loving passion for souls still to this day. God wants to listen to the sincere confession of the man who loves God and his neighbor as himself. God uses men of love the most. There is love in the inner motivation of every one who devotes himself joyfully and faithfully.

Blessing Received on the Way That the Lord Said to Go

During the time I was a chaplain in the Air Force, I prayed, "Let all the people of this country become believers of Jesus."

God taught me an unforgettable lesson. After wrapping up my time as an associate pastor, I began my first ministry as a chaplain to serve at Mt. Ilwol. My first Sunday, I went to church with a trembling heart and great expectations, but to my disappointment, there was no one in the chapel. I began to ask around why this was happening and found out that there were certain circumstances that did not allow the soldiers to join the service on Sundays. I was so disappointed when I found this out. The only thing I could do was to cry at the pulpit.

"Father, why did you send me to this kind of place? Why did you bring me here? I prayed for the complete evangelization of all the soldiers!"

I was so disappointed and heartbroken that I prayed earnestly to God every day. I did not know why He sent me where there was not even a single true believer. I could not even dream about the whole troop's evangelization but was deeply grateful even when a few soldiers showed up to the service each week. So I could not just leave from the pulpit, but threw myself crying before the Lord and prayed. "Lord, change all the soldiers through the Gospel."

I don't know exactly how long I prayed, but suddenly I heard God's voice.

"Do you really want to make all the soldiers become believers?"

I paid close attention to His voice.

"To save just you alone, I had to leave my throne of Heaven to come to this earth and even die on the cross. If you wished for all soldiers to be saved, do you know how many sacrifices you must make to save all the soldiers?"

The word of the Lord felt like he was asking me if I could die for the soldiers to save them. Tears rushed down my face. After calming myself down a bit, I confessed to God.

"For evangelization of all soldiers, Lord, I am willing to die. It is okay for me to die, so please help all soldiers to believe in Jesus."

After that day, I decided to give my life for evangelization of all the soldiers. I promised the Lord that I would sacrifice for them even if I would become a martyr. It meant that I would give my all for Jesus.

First I shared my decision with my wife and asked for her understanding. "Honey, I'm sorry, but please take the children and go to your parents' house."

In this way, my little children who did not know anything went to live in their grandparents' house. I felt very sorry for my family as a husband and as a father. Fortunately, my wife's family was financial stable, so I didn't even give her my salary as chaplain during this period of time. "Please live at your parents' house for a while, having meals from your parents."

I spent all my income on the soldiers. Before I went in the Military Official Residence, I was living in my own housing, so I was rather free to visit the soldiers. I went around the area of Mt. Ilwol around one or two in the morning and started to evangelize soldiers who were keeping watch. My strategy was *love*. I brewed coffee and brought cookies to give them. I tried to serve them with a heart like serving my elder and younger brothers. Actually, after seeing soldiers who were not able to sleep and were keeping watch on cold winter nights, I identified with them. I visited them with a compassionate heart and shared hot coffee and something to eat, encouraging them, saying, "Thank you for your hard work."

Maybe it was well accepted. When they finished eating the food I brought for them, they did not reject my request. "I would like to pray for you, may I pray?"

It was the time so called "'Yoo-shin.'"[8] In this situation, it was very dangerous to go around that particular area of the mountain at midnight. If I was recognized as a man of suspicious character, I would have probably been shot and killed right on the spot. But there was nothing for me to fear since I already made a decision to die for God. I was already filled with the boldness God had granted to me.

One week after I reached the soldiers in this way, there were about ten soldiers who attended the worship service on Sunday. But something extraordinary happened. The most famous and intimidating commanding

---

[8] A period under military dictatorship during the 1970s in Korea when the time of ideological conflict was serious.

officer came to the military church. I saluted him with honor and asked, "How did you come here, sir?"

"I'm here for worship."

"Welcome sir, come in, please."

Upon the commanding officer's arrival at the chapel, everyone raised their hands to salute him. The commanding officer took a quick look around.

"Why are there just a few soldiers here?"

"What do you mean? There were not even this many people a while ago."

This was the reason why the commanding officer came to the chapel. He had received reports from the security force that the new chaplain was suspiciously going around the base without sleeping at night. So he gave an order to investigate what the pastor was doing at night. I'm sure my background and bio had been reported to him as well. The investigation result was obvious. The pastor supplied food and coffee to soldiers on night duty and prayed for them every day. That's all.

After receiving the report, I believe the commanding officer was moved greatly by the Holy Spirit. He was so touched that he himself voluntarily visited the chapel. I guess he was so dissatisfied with the empty seats around the chapel that he went to the duty office and gave an order to the officer of the day. "All the soldiers, come to the chapel in five minutes!"

Five minutes! Exactly within five minutes, all the soldiers gathered in the chapel. The famous, intimidating commanding officer was known as a "tiger" around the base camp. He had punished even staff officers severely in front of all the soldiers in the past, so when the soldiers heard his order, all of them ran to the chapel. Some soldiers came running out of breath and didn't even have time to lace their boots. All but a few of the soldiers who were outside of the base gathered at the chapel.

That day was recorded as the first worship with all the soldiers at the base camp. The chapel seemed so small that when all the soldiers came in, it felt like the chapel was going to burst. So after the worship, I asked all the squad leaders to stay.

"When soldiers on an outing come back, there is no way for all of us to fit in the chapel for Wednesday service. Please pick the time and the place for worship so I can go to every squad and lead services there."

After that time, I led twenty-six worship services a week. My lips were blistered every day from having to lead all the worship services. But it was my honor and joy. After these events, the commanding officer decided on the goal for the following year without even consulting me. "The next year's goal of our corps is for all the soldiers to be believers."

Ever since the commanding officer set the goal for the corps, he often gave a sudden order through the base broadcasting system in the middle of the day. "All the officers in the base camp come to the headquarters office."

I was also an officer at that time, so when I heard the announcement, I ran as fast as I could. When I arrived, I was suddenly given orders to lead a Bible study for all the officers.

Since then, noncommissioned officers had their own Bible studies, and the soldiers were also gathered to have a Bible study of their own. I became extremely busy because of all these Bible studies that were being held around the base. Every day, I had a blessed military life, shouting a happy cheer, especially, one year when I shared the Four Spiritual Laws with every single soldier in the corps; it was a time where my heart was moved and filled with gratitude each day.

After a year, the corps decided to hold a baptismal ceremony for all of its soldiers. A baptism service for the entire corps! It was the first time ever in the history of the Air Force. On the day of baptism, I could not help but give all the glory and praise to God who performed this miracle.

Looking back, I am astonished that I saw these kinds of miracles in my pastoral ministry wherever I went. The Lord did everything. All I did was make up my mind even to die for this ministry, but the Holy Spirit accomplished all things directly by sending the right people. Therefore, I have nothing to boast about.

The following year, I was relocated to Busan. The Army had previously recorded the evangelization of the entire troops before; however, it was the first time in the history of the Air Force to have evangelization of the entire corps. So it was special treatment from the chief chaplain to relocate me to the place that I wished to go. I was asked, "Where do you want to go? I'll send you wherever you want to go."

During that period, there was a famous elder named Tae-Sung Jung at Cho-Ryang Church in Busan. What caught my attention was that he was the chairman of the Military Evangelism Committee. I thought I would have the chance to reach the entire military in Busan if I worked together with him, so I told the chief chaplain that I wanted to go to Busan. The Holy Spirit was already pouring this burning love and passion toward the city of Busan into my heart. Without the Holy Spirit's help, there was no possible way for me to grow such interest and passion for the evangelization of the entire military in Busan out of the many other areas.

The whole time I spent as a chaplain in Busan, it looked like I was dreaming. It was one of the happiest periods of my life. Not only was the entire military evangelized, but also I lived receiving much support, love, and care from many churches in Busan. The church in the base was so filled with the Holy Spirit that civil officials, commissioned officers, civilians, and their wives came to join the services. The entire base was like a field of the pastoral ministry. The officer in charge of church finances was one of the deacons in the church. He collected membership fees regularly from everyone on salary day. Therefore, the finances of our church were always overflowing. Whenever they would hold troop-wide soccer games, the church would provide the food and drinks, whether our team won or lost. The chief commander of transportation sometimes made the soldiers stand in a line and wait for me to come, so that I could pray for them before they began their day. The officers and their wives served in the choir, and all the soldiers came to church to praise God every Sunday.

The news of what had happened in the military chapel spread outside of the military base. The Christian Businessman's Committee sent me a message saying that they would support constructing a church building in the military base before I got discharged. I never made a request, but they suggested it.

Everything worked out in such a manner. When I was serving as an associate pastor, someone told me that he would build a church in the Kang-Nam area in Seoul. Sooyoungro Church was also built by an elder of Choryang Church, so I started to plant the church. Therefore, I have no merit on my part. Who could not do the pastoral ministry well if somebody else constructs the church building and provides honoraria! The Lord did everything. The only thing I did was to seek the

Lord's will, wait, and make a decision to follow. God told me to go, so I went, and great blessings beyond my imagination were always already prepared.

The Man of God Is the One with a Heart Burning with Love

The majority of the Lord's servants consider how they can improve their capabilities before doing pastoral ministry. They think about how they can receive many more abilities from God. On the other side of these thoughts are their imaginations of becoming a wonderful pastor, who works in many ways for the Lord with these great abilities and many skills. However, before they begin their wonderful ministry, there is something God requires first. There is something one must prepare first. "Are you ready in your mind to sacrifice with love? Are you ready to serve the Lord, surrendering all you have?"

The Lord asks these things. What is important in God's eyes is our attitude of surrendering everything for the sake of God's kingdom and His righteousness and still regretting nothing. God sees first whether we love Him so much that we can die for Him and whether we are willing to love the entrusted sheep to the point of death.

Therefore, before expecting God's blessing or glory through our pastoral ministry, we should be ready to suffer for the sake of love. Second, whether there is a crown or no crown should be left to the Lord's will, and we must examine ourselves first to see whether we are ready to endure the suffering of bearing the cross for the sake of the souls and to run for the Kingdom of God. This is the best preparatory work for the pastoral ministry.

"Where should I go for You, Lord? What should I do for You, Lord? What should I give for you today, Lord?" We must have this kind of burning heart of love. The one who has that kind of heart is truly part of the called. On the contrary, if you are concerned with, "How can I succeed in the pastoral ministry? How can I become famous? What can I do to make them serve me well?," then you are just a wage-earning shepherd. If you are a pastor, you should examine whether or not you are truly called by God. If one does not have the slightest readiness of heart—namely, if you are not ready in your mind to love and sacrifice—then such a person is clearly the one who does not have the calling.

I do not mean the asceticism of Catholicism when I say to be prepared to suffer. It is not "suffering for suffering," nor "suffering for Buddhist emancipation." It is to sacrifice because of love for the soul. It means that we must regard our time, our money, and our pride as excrement. We must be ready to throw ourselves for the Lord and to love the flocks entrusted to us by the Lord. The one who entrusts himself completely to the Lord lives as if lacking common sense. This kind of person makes an abundant offering though he does not have enough, is willing to work for the Lord though he is busy, and does the ministry without fear in spite of danger. Sometimes, he makes strange decisions. He chooses a difficult and hard path instead of an easy and well-paved way.

But what is strange? Although we chose the very narrow and hard way, if the Lord pours His grace, we receive the most glorious and glittering blessings from the Lord. This is the principle of life in the Kingdom of God.

"Seek first His kingdom and His righteousness, and all these things will be given to you as well" (Matthew 6:33).

A few years ago, when I looked at my bank account to see if I had money saved up for my daughter's wedding, I realized I did not have any. Even my daughter did not trust the fact that I did not have money.

"Mom, is it true we don't have money?"

Surely, Sooyoungro Church gives me a sufficient honorarium. It is rare to find a pastor whose salary is as high as mine. For this, I always feel like I owed much to many other pastors. Since the Lord of money is God, my wife and I were the same in giving to God first. Perhaps my wife is stricter than I am in this area.

As the church grew bigger, the number of people requesting help increased. Please do not misunderstand. I never meant that I make tremendous sacrifices for them. My food and clothes have been taken care of by the church. Many people in the church serve for this insufficient servant, and because of these people, I do not have to worry about food and living. I have enough clothes and shoes.

I have no reason to save money because I have enough. First of all, it was I who made the confession that I could even die for God when I was young, and I did not want to save money and to have my heart rely on the money that I had. Though I was not taught how to manage money in a Christian household, God himself taught me the priorities on money management through moving my heart by the Holy Spirit. When money came in, He led me to give it to God first and to use the rest for the Lord.

My wife was better at this than I. Although my wife was raised in a wealthy family, after she married me, she preceded me in giving. One day after we were married, a distant relative stayed in my house and importunately asked us for money for several days. During that time, my wife was fasting in prayer. However, she was not only cooking to serve every meal for him, but also finally gave him the only one bankbook. The bankbook was given by her parents when she married this poor seminary student. But my wife gave it to the poor relative who was pestering for money.

Later on, she confessed that she had only looked at a distant mountain for several days since then. I could understand her feelings because whenever times were difficult, she took the bankbook and looked at it quietly. However, in a sense, she purposefully gave the bankbook to the poor relative because she did not want to depend on money more than God. Perhaps she felt that it was time for her to decide to give away everything freely to people in need. Ever since this incident, my wife has used the money ungrudgingly to give to God and to help the people in need.

"No one can serve two masters. Either he will hate the one and love the other, or he will be devoted to the one and despise the other. You cannot serve both God and money" (Matthew 6:24).

Yet my wife and I do not live like ascetics. We have a better house than we deserve, more abundant and delicious food than we deserve, better clothes than we deserve, and are overwhelmed always. We live and enjoy life just like the descendants of God's royal family. We say we give much to God, but even the things that we give are from God. We also live in abundance through the things that are gifts from God. Therefore, there is nothing to boast of as our meritorious deed. I am not saying that it is always right to live without a savings account like us. What I want to say is that God wants us who are abundantly blessed to live sharing and giving what we have instead of saving.

After realizing my family's financial circumstance before my daughter's wedding, I called and asked the pastor, the father of the groom, about their financial situation. However, their family's financial situation was worse than ours. They had saved some money for their son's wedding, but they gave all the savings to the church because of an emergency situation that the church was facing. They did not even have a million won (about one thousand and one hundred US dollars in 2014 exchange rate). I said joyfully, "Well, it's okay! We don't have money either. Let's just become in-laws by having the wedding ceremony in the amount that we have!"

Despite the circumstances, the wedding ceremony was done very well. The elders of the church discussed this matter themselves and helped to hold a great wedding ceremony. I refused with appreciation continually, but the elders let the ceremony move onward with great rapidity. The elders of Sooyoungro Church served this inefficient servant heartily beyond my imagination.

It may sound like boasting, but as I experience these kinds of incidents, I become more convinced that when God's children surrender everything to God, giving their most sincere heart and effort as well as their belongings and body in serving God, He gives abundant rewards to His children abundantly, tenfold or a hundredfold. When His children surrender themselves to serve God without expecting any rewards, God rewards them abundantly and gives them the shining crowns.

The problem should be, "Do I confess my sincere confession of love to God?" To His children who make this confession, God the Father will crown them with the crown of blessing.

I know one pastor who lived as an evangelist for his entire life. However, the fruit of the pastoral ministry was fruitless. Although, he lived only working for evangelism every day, incredibly he had almost no fruits.

Nevertheless, he never became discouraged and continuously went out to evangelize every day. With love for Christ, he obeyed God's commandments every day and proclaimed the Gospel. Because of his commitment, his wife had to carry all the burden of raising the children. However, their children were all raised incredibly well. Not only was their faith and character outstanding, but also they are blessed to be financial plutocrats. What is more joyful than seeing our kids grow up well, being influential people? When we nestle in the bosom of our Lord, the clearest traces we can leave here on earth are children.

I have learned and been impressed greatly watching his life. What God looks at the most is not "How many souls we have saved?" or "How big have we done the pastoral ministry?" Rather, what God looks at as the most important thing is to work completely to the end obeying the Lord's commandment and to live for the Lord until the end, loving the Lord. I realized that God awards the greatest prize to us when we demonstrate our confession of love for God through our life every day. Also, I recognized that God awards us with the greatest reward at the right time when the rewards are provided. It is important that although we are disappointed by no visible fruits, eventually we realize God's grace that allows us to reap the harvest of joy. Whether you are a pastor or a laity, doing God's work itself is already a big award. In that sense, the third stanza of hymn number 260 from the Korean Hymnal touches my heart deeply.

Going forth with weeping, sowing for the Master,
Tho' the loss sustained our spirit often grieves;
When our weeping's over, He will bid us welcome,
We shall come, rejoicing, bringing in the sheaves.
Bringing in the sheaves, bringing in the sheaves,

We shall come, rejoicing, bringing in the sheaves.
Bringing in the sheaves, bringing in the sheaves,
We shall come, rejoicing, bringing in the sheaves.

We do not know how God will lead our lives or our pastoral ministries. All things are done by the Holy Spirit, and God will receive the glory. If so, what are we supposed to do? We have to give a confession of love! For the Lord and for the sheep entrusted by the Lord, one thing we have to do is simply to lift up our confession of love that we will do everything at the risk of our lives. With that confession we have to live day by day. This is the best life.

Love More, Work More!

Elisha, Elijah's disciple, asked a double portion of Elijah's spirit before he ascended to heaven.

"When they had crossed, Elijah said to Elisha, 'Tell me, what can I do for you before I am taken from you?' 'Let me inherit a double portion of your spirit'" (2 Kings 2:9).

Then Elijah replied, "You have asked a difficult thing" (2 Kings 2:10).

Why did Elijah reply so to Elisha? Since nothing is impossible for God, it is not too difficult for God to give a double portion of the spirit to Elisha. But why did Elijah say, "You have asked a difficult thing?"

It was not that it was difficult for God to give a double portion of the spirit, but it meant that Elisha's life would be much more difficult if he were to receive a double portion of the spirit. To receive that much portion of spirit means that he has to give up everything in his life and carry out God's work with sacrifice and effort. In other words, it means, "You are volunteering for a very difficult path."

I also pray, "Please give me a sevenfold portion of Elijah's spirit," feeling this last generation is more evil and lewd than the times of Elisha. My congregation also prays the same prayer. "Please make our pastor to be a servant, going to preach in the five oceans and in the six continents."

But imagine if the prayer is to be answered. If I were to receive a sevenfold portion of Elijah's spirit, can I live even eating a meal comfortably? How much will I be tired and busy? Let me explain more easily! When I pray putting my hands on AIDS patients and if they all are healed, then wherever I go, how many patients and needy people will come to me? Maybe I do not have time to sleep. People will run after me day and night wherever I go. Plus, I will use such power only given by God, and I cannot even make money like fortunetellers. Moreover, even if I receive money, what can I do? In a word, will I be in a bad fix?

This is a simple example. Very often, we do not know what it means to ask God for the power. The power of God and inspiration of God are given in any way to do the work of God. Therefore, when we ask for God's inspiration, there has to be a commitment that we will love more and dedicate more. In other words, it has to be with the confession, "I will die more for you, Lord."

Likewise, when we pray for more growth in our parish or our church, we must be aware of the exact meaning of the prayer. When the heart genuinely confesses to love more and work more, a revival will follow. When more flocks are gathered, so much more will our tasks and distressing burdens increase. As the Korean proverb says, "For the tree with many branches, there are no days the wind goes down." The more children you have, although there are many good things, the more worries and troubles the parents face. Like this when the church grows more, there are many good things; however, many problems also appear. As Sooyoungro Church has grown, the number of associate ministers has also increased. It is not easy to manage and serve the number of associate ministers. If just one pastor has problems, hundreds of church members are affected. As the church is growing, works and tasks to be done increase. More dedicated people must appear. When we cry out to the Lord, "Please revive us," God rather asks us, "Do you want to dedicate yourself that much?"

There is a similar story in the Bible.

"Then the mother of Zebedee's sons came to Jesus with her sons and, kneeling down, asked a favor of him. 'What is it you want?' he asked. She said, 'Grant that one of these two sons of mine may sit at your right and the other at your left in your kingdom'" (Matthew 20:20–21).

How did the Lord respond to this request?

"'You don't know what you are asking,' Jesus said to them. 'Can you drink the cup I am going to drink?'" (Matthew 20:22).

We humans imagine only the glorious figure to sit at the right and left side of the Lord becoming a great servant of the Lord. However, the Lord tells us to first understand what it means to seek after such glory. That is, if we want to receive the great glory, we must pass through the cross first.

What is the meaning of carrying the cross? It has many meanings, but first of all, it means to throw away the comforts of the world, wealth, fame, and the desire for power for the Lord. Also, it means we accept the hardship when we throw away such things. That is the first step of bearing the cross.

"If anyone comes to me and does not hate father and mother, wife and children, brothers and sisters—yes, even their own life—such a person cannot be my disciple . . . In the same way, those of you who do not give up everything you have cannot be my disciples" (Luke 14:26, 33).

In the Old Testament, we can find out that even a great prophet ran away in fear of martyrdom and complained to God about his suffering. As humans, who would not be afraid of such persecution and suffering? It is painful for everyone to bear the cross. However, when we confess the love for Jesus, yet if we do not bear the cross, we cannot follow the way that Jesus went.

Thomas A. Kempis says in his famous book *Imitation of Christ,* "Christians can't run away from the cross. He is not a follower of Christ anymore if he avoids the cross. Even when Christians run outside, there is the cross. Even when we hide inside, you'll find the cross there. The cross is waiting for us when we go up or go down." When Christians make up their minds to trust in Jesus truly, it means that the cross is surely waiting for all of us.

This is a story about a female deacon in the countryside of Korea. For several reasons, she was having a difficult life in faith. As a result, whenever she prayed, she cried out, "Lord, it is too hard!"

One night she had a dream. She was walking laboriously, dragging a big cross. Just at that time, Jesus appeared to her. So she begged, "Lord, You are a carpenter. This cross is too heavy. So, please cut a little bit." Jesus smiled at her and cut the cross a little bit. She continued the walk and again, she felt like her cross was still too heavy. She begged again, looking at the cross, "Please cut a little bit more." Every time she proceeded, she asked the Lord to cut out the cross a little bit more.

Whenever she asked, Jesus accepted her request and cut off the cross more and more.

Finally, she arrived at the gate of heaven. When she looked around, everyone had their own cross and they received rewards based on the size of the cross. She took a look at her cross and was so shocked. Her own cross became small enough to fit in her hand. At that moment, she woke up. While she was praying, at least she realized why Jesus had said, "If anyone would come after me, he must deny himself and take up his cross and follow me."

Heaven is already guaranteed for us because we believe in Jesus Christ. But there will be no rewards if we enter heaven simply as a person who was blessed and had a peaceful life. Therefore, it is not the blessed one, but rather the very foolish one, as one who enters into heaven never making an effort, never dedicated, and never giving up anything for God.

The Apostles were pleased, considering it joy and an honor when they were beaten and put in prison due to their proclamation of the Gospel. They already knew the secret of the reward they would receive in heaven.

"The Spirit himself testifies with our spirit that we are God's children. Now if we are children, then we are heirs—heirs of God and co-heirs with Christ, if indeed we share in his sufferings in order that we may also share in his glory. I consider that our present sufferings are not worth comparing with the glory that will be revealed in us" (Romans 8:16–18).

Still today, God is searching for people who are willing to carry the cross because of their love for God.

God intensely pays attention to those who bear the cross joyfully with appreciation and gratitude. Do you really want to do the work of the Lord? Seek first the cross. We must seek the love of the cross and the sacrifice of the cross. Without the cross, there is no crown.

CHAPTER 4

Prayer: The Sanctuary Will Be Filled When Tears Are Filled

God Hears the Prayer of the Humble

Since my childhood, I had made up my mind to be a pastor, though I never thought for a moment that I would plant a church and work the pastoral ministry at the church. How difficult it is to plant a church! Actually, I was quite introverted and timid. Therefore, I was thinking that I was far from a church planter, and it would be difficult for me to even be a pastor. When I realized this, I prayed to God seriously, asking if it would not be better for me to live as a laity. God, however, spoke to me clearly that I will walk the path of a pastor. Ever since I heard His voice, even though it was desperate when I looked at myself, I started my journey as a pastor with conviction that if God was with me, I could be used as well.

Before I planted a church, God made me realize through numerous training courses, that it was the Holy Spirit doing the pastoral ministries. God also helped me realize how pastors should serve God as their Lord in the field of pastoral ministry. God himself who accepted my inadequacy was guiding and leading me in person. The first course was at seminary. I was very disappointed when I entered the seminary right after graduating college. Most of the academic curriculum was in the process of being stabilized, so the system overall was very disorganized. Therefore, it was not the right circumstance to study theological study systematically. A passion to study was not found anywhere in the school. I was so discouraged that I even felt stupid for making the decision to take the three-year course of theological study.

Once again, with an anxious heart I knelt before God. Problems I never faced at the prestigious schools before gave me an indescribably heavy feeling. In such situations, my heart was very heavy. However, this happened because pride entered my mind.

While I was praying, God again helped me realize the pride in me. God also taught me the fact that I could be ruined by being crashed into a rock of pride during the three years in the seminary, as well as the fact that it would be a success for me if I stayed the course for three years at the seminary without bumping into the rock of pride. Was it my ability that I was able to graduate from such prestigious schools where students study very hard? It was possible only because God endowed me with such wisdom. We human beings can become fools suddenly if God withdraws His wisdom. Does a pastor's competence of pastoral ministry and an evaluation of who he is before God come from our intellectual ability and educational background? Many pastors engaged in the ministry neglect this fact. Therefore, very often, a large number of pastors try to work the ministry through their own capability and intelligence.

Pastoral ministry is done not with knowledge or capability, but with humility. God's blessings are poured out when we carry out the ministry with humility. Thus, humility is real capability and competence of the pastoral ministry.

When my mind began to realize this point, I decided not to focus my energy on the diploma and title. I thought that it was not necessary to achieve the diploma anymore. Pastors, of course, should be lifelong learners, but their purpose should be to feed their flock of sheep well, not to judge others or to make themselves high.

Pride is to evaluate things that God must do and to take the glory that God must take. Pride is also to think something that we do not need to think about. Pride starts to sprout when we do not fully understand our identity. People often are caught by pride because of a little title, a little achievement, and a little thought.

Take a look at the example of the righteous man Job in the Bible. While he was in the midst of suffering, three of his friends devoted themselves to arguments. While the righteous Job was listening to the arguments, eventually he also got involved in the dispute. Being involved in the arguments means his thought became conceited as well. That moment, God appeared to Job, who then recognized his ignorance. Even such a righteous man was rebuked by God.

> "Who is this that darkens my counsel with words without knowledge? Brace yourself like a man; I will question you, and you shall answer me. Where were you when I laid the earth's foundation? Tell

me if you understand. Who marked off its dimensions? Surely you know! Who stretched measuring lines across it? On what were its footings set, or who laid its cornerstone—while the morning stars sang together and all the angels shouted for joy? Who shut up the sea behind doors when it burst forth from the womb, when I made the clouds its garment and wrapped it in thick darkness, when I fixed limits for it and set its doors and bars in place, when I said, 'This far you may come and no further; here is where your proud waves halt'? Have you ever given orders to the morning, or shown the dawn its place?" (Job 38:2–12).

What is man? In the end, man is only a creature. It is really ridiculous that the creature became arrogant before the Creator. The Lord said to Job, "You, Job! If you are really smart, have you ever commanded for morning and let the sun arise?"

By that time, Job realized his own identity and repented of his sin to become humble before God again. "I am unworthy—how can I reply to you? I put my hand over my mouth. I spoke once, but I have no answer—twice, but I will say no more" (Job 40:4–5).

What happened to Job after that? Job, who became humble again, received double portions of blessings from God. God is looking for a man of humility. He does not tolerate arrogant people.

A role model for many pastors, D. L. Moody, only attended elementary school. Due to that, he was often corrected of his wrong use of words and pronunciations during his sermon. But there were no other revivalists who were used more by God than Moody. It is said that in his life through his Gospel rallies, he led more than a million souls to Christ. How was this possible? How did he become a tool that the Holy Spirit had used?

It was his humility. He was said to be a man of outright humility. Because he lacked a level of intellect due to only finishing the fourth grade in elementary school, he was even more completely humble before God. He confessed throughout his life that he had no power or any good thing that would change and inspire people. Therefore, he utterly relied on the Holy Spirit. Recognizing that there was nothing to boast in his own ability, in his own academic capability, and in his own thought, he wholeheartedly relied only on the Holy Spirit. Then the explosive work of the Spirit took place wherever he went. The Holy Spirit was able to freely use Moody who humbly entrusted himself to the Holy Spirit.

By doing the work of the Lord, ministers are objects whom God looks at preciously. But once we make an effort, once we bear the cross, and once we try to proclaim the Gospel, would we rather become a tool being used totally by the Holy Spirit just like Moody? The principle of God's kingdom is thus paradoxical. When I become the smaller, God becomes the greater. And when I die, the Spirit becomes alive. When I become humble, the work of the Holy Spirit prospers.

The absolute obedience for humility! It was the assignment and issue given to me by God for the three years in seminary. God was asking me so that I do not become conceited in my thinking or in my life because I am nothing. Pastoral ministry is done not with knowledge but with humility. Therefore, the Lord wanted to teach me that a humble pastor always clings completely on God through prayer. I believe that the reason I had a chance to serve a newly planted church in my second year in the seminary was because of such intention to the Lord. God called me, a second-year seminary student, to serve for a newly planted church as pastor, to be a pastor who completely lives a life of prayer.

When Prayers Are Filled with Tears, the Church Will Be Filled with People

When I was in my second year in seminary, some deacons from a newly planted church came to me and asked if I could preach on Sundays as an interim pastor because the church had no senior pastor. From that time on, I started to preach for that church's Sunday worship, Sunday afternoon worship, Wednesday evening worship, and seven days of dawn prayer meetings. That meant I had to lead ten worship services per week. I had never worked before as an intern pastor, but now it looked like I had already started pastoral ministry with about thirty members.

Due to this sudden church planting ministry entrusted to me, I had to cry out before God every day. I cried before God, first of all asking His provision of the Word of God to feed the flock of sheep given to me. As a second-year seminary student, it was beyond my capability to prepare ten sermons each week. But God looked upon this insufficient man with His loving eyes and allowed the church to grow steadily. When I delivered a sermon from the pulpit, the congregation responded with "Amen," and new believers were increasing every week.

One Sunday around 1976 while I was preaching, I saw a newcomer sitting in the back seat. At that time, many people in the rural areas were moving to Seoul. The newcomer also gave the impression that she had also recently moved from the country side. She was noticeable because she was constantly nodding at my sermon. It was a sign that she had been blessed.

After the service, she approached me while I was exchanging greetings with the members of the church at the doorway in the back.

"*Jeondosanim*[9] (Minister), from now on I want to attend this church continually."

Then she registered as a member of the church. She was a deacon from Daegoo, about my mother's age and very diligent and earnest in her prayer life. Her nickname was "Captain of Prayer" like she could be called a prophet; she was living an ardent and clear life before the Lord. Her membership to our church became a big help and provided vitality for the pastoral ministry on the church planting process. Above all, through her appearance, I was able to do the home visitation ministry of the church members positively because I was single at that time. Thankfully, she was very stable financially and she was older, so she was not so busy. She was my co-worker sent by the Lord. She helped me like a mother, visiting church member's houses with this poor single minister, providing taxi fares as well as lunches. I, therefore, was able to visit our members' homes as often as I could without worrying about anything. I was so happy. It really felt like God sent an angel to assist my ministry.

She also was very happy every day. One day we were on our way out from visiting a member's house, and I noticed that she wasn't walking behind me. So

---

[9] In the Korean church, there are several different levels of minister. In this case, "minister" originally means *Jeondosa*. Here, *Jeondosa* is a student minister who is serving for a local church as a seminary student. Sometimes, a *Jeondosa* is a man or woman minister who serves in a local church as part of a ministerial staff who has not been ordained.

I looked back. She was standing under an old tree, looking up to the sky with her eyes closed softly. I asked her, "Deacon, what are you doing there?"

She answered, "Minister, I have been truly blessed! I am just wondering if this is a dream or reality."

Even though a seminary student delivered the messages, she received them with great gratitude. She was truly a humble woman. Because she confessed such happiness every day, she often delayed her time to return home.

"Minister, can we visit one more family?"

Visiting church member homes with a person who deeply sought the grace of God was truly joyful and happy.

At that time I realized that the pastor ministry must be like this. The pastoral ministry can be identified with a state where my co-worker feels happy because of me, and I feel happy as well because of them. My secretaries who help me feel happy due to the senior pastor, and the senior pastor is happy due to his staff—this is the real pastoral ministry. Although a pastor preaches happiness, peace and joy, if there is no peace and joy in the actual pastoral ministerial field, how can we explain the situation?

I was able to experience and learn how I should work together with co-workers in the ministry through serving with her. The lessons I learned from her have been the backbone of my pastoral ministry throughout my life. One day, she asked me suddenly, "Minister, do you want your church to be completely filled with people?"

I replied with my eyes wide open. "Well, do you need to ask that? Of course, I want my church to be filled."

Then she responded, "Only when tears, tears of prayers, are filled up here at the church, the church will be filled up with people. It is that much difficult to fill the church with people."

My initial reaction to her comment was, "Well, what? You are saying something too strange! How do I fill the church with my tears even if I cry for the rest of my life?"

But strangely, the words of the deacon would not leave my mind as time passed from that moment.

"Tears, tears of prayer, are to be filled here at the church. Then the church can be filled up with people. Filled with tears, then the church. . . ."

Since these words would not leave my mind, I thought the Lord gave these words. So, from that night forward I started all-night prayers.

I began to cry before the pulpit thinking like this: "Though my tears of prayer cannot be filled up at the church, perhaps I may be able to fill this one small pulpit with my tears of prayer."

With this idea I started to cry and realized, "I must cry as much as I can."

As long as I made that decision, I prayed, shedding all the tears possible. I prayed for God to save the dying souls, for God to send more sheep to my church, for God to give me the words, and for God to bless the flock of sheep already coming to our church. After I prayed for a while, I then turned myself 90 degrees and started praying again in tears. I wanted to fill up the pulpit with my tears. I prayed all night turning to the windows and also turning to the congregation.

On the following day, I prayed sitting in a different location.

"God, please fill this sanctuary with people!"

With this request, I prayed all night, turning to every side of the sanctuary. Like the deacon said, if a church is filled with people when the tears in prayers are filled up, I thought the church should not be empty because I was

94

lacking tears in my prayers. Could it happen because I thought this way? Strangely, tears always fell from my eyes ever since I felt determined to pray in tears.

Then a truly amazing thing happened. Three months after I started serving at the church, the attendance of the church rose to 105 people. The sanctuary was packed and was too small for Sunday worship! We had to move to a bigger facility, and the same thing happened three times that year. When the church moved to a bigger place, it became too small right away.

Moving again and again, one day I checked the attendance of the Sunday worship when I was about to graduate from seminary. The attendance was about 160–170 people. I realized that the words of the deacon were not wrong. Also, I came to understand a little bit more about the identity of a pastor. Who is the pastor? The pastor is the one who weeps while embracing the souls. The pastor is the one who fills up the sanctuary with tears.

Ask Persistently until Your Prayer Is Answered

There are many commanding and encouraging words to pray in many places of the Bible. One example can be found in Luke 11:5–13, a story about a man who was traveling and came to the house of a friend in the middle of the night. He was starving, but there was no food in the house. So the host went to one of his closest friends who was his neighbor and knocked on the door to ask for three pieces of bread. But the problem was timing. It was in the middle of the night. The neighbor was already asleep with his children. When he awoke from the loud knocking noise, he was even more upset when he found out that it was his friend next door.

"What a man this is! Does he know what time it is right now? How rude is this man? I will have to handle this tomorrow."

The friend who was very upset might have complained like this. But the one who knocked on the door would not give up and return home. He desperately wanted to obtain three pieces of bread to feed his hungry friend who was traveling. So he continued banging on the door shamelessly. Watching over the situation from his bed, the neighbor finally got up from his bed and gave him what he wanted because he thought that this man would continue to knock on the door all night until his demand was met.

"I tell you, though he will not get up and give him the bread because he is his friend, yet because of the man's boldness he will get up and give him as much as he needs" (Luke 11:8).

When telling this story, Jesus said in verse 9, "So I say to you: Ask and it will be given to you; seek and you will find; knock and the door will be open to you. For everyone who asks receives; he who seeks finds; and to him who knocks, the door will be opened" (Luke 11:9–10).

It means you must shamelessly persist when praying. Tears often follow when we pray persistently. Although you know sometimes it is very shameful to ask, when you have to pray because it is necessary, tears are most likely pouring out.

Hannah and Hezekiah demonstrated this fact very well. Hannah prayed to God with tears, pouring out her heart before God because of her difficult situation: "In her deep anguish Hannah prayed to the Lord, weeping bitterly" (1 Samuel 1:10).

When Hezekiah was diagnosed with a fatal disease, he prayed, weeping loudly to God. Then God answered him promptly.

"Go back and tell Hezekiah, the leader of my people, 'this is what the Lord, the God of your father David, says: I have heard your prayer and seen your tears; I will heal you. On the third day from now you will go up to the temple of the Lord" (2 Kings 20:5).

Likewise, God highly values prayers in tears. Our heavenly father cannot help but answer prayer when we are praying fretfully with tears. But selfish prayers to satisfy one's greed cannot be answered, no matter how hard you pray in tears. Even if you pray for a long time, your prayer will never be answered if it is for worldly ambition.

"When you ask, you do not receive, because you ask with wrong motives, that you may spend what you get on your pleasures" (James 4:3).

Those who ask with wrong motives are like those who bow down before idols. Thus, a man of prayer should have a clear answer the following questions: How shall I live if God answers my prayers? How shall I serve God? What shall I do for God?

If the prayer of a person who asks according to his lustful desire is answered, he will commit even bigger sins because of the answer. He will be more depraved than before. Therefore, the more important thing than "to be answered quickly" is "how will I live for God when my prayer is answered?"

So Hannah made a vow, wailing as she prayed: "And she made a vow, saying, 'O Lord Almighty, if you will only look upon your servant's misery and remember me, and not forget your servant but give her a son, then I will give him to the Lord for all the days of his life, and no razor will ever be used on his head" (1 Samuel 1:11). A prayer of vow is not a like making a deal. It is not the same concept as "If you do this for me, I will do that for you." It is complete self-devotion and commitment. Hannah must have had many thoughts as she saw Peninnah, who agitated her by giving birth to a child first. She may have realized how wicked it is before the Lord to give pain to a childless mother by boasting about her children. She may have thought, if she gave birth to a child, she would raise her child not for her own pride, but for the glory of Jehovah. Perhaps she might realize that it was the most blessed and beautiful way through her long wait. At any rate, in her long period of waiting, Hannah made a vow that she would dedicate her child to God. It was a decision of life. Hannah did not pray, "If you answer my prayer, I will raise the child well. Then I will put down Peninnah absolutely." Rather she prayed with a vow, "If God allows me a child, I will dedicate my child to God." It was a prayer of her decision that she would focus on in her life.

"God, I have lived only for myself until now. I am ill. Now I finally realize how futile and empty my life had been. If you restore me, I will devote my life not for the empty life, but for the eternal God, Jehovah. I will use all of my time and possession for you, Lord. Because I realized that it is the most blessed life. If you heal me Lord, I will tithe out of all my possession first, and I will use one tenth of my time serving for the Lord's church."

This kind of vow is a resolution of one's faith that one will give one's life completely to the Lord.

God sees our hidden motives. He is the Holy Spirit. Therefore, God knows very well the hidden motives in our prayer for revival of the church, whether it is for our glory or for God's glory, and whether answering the prayer will lead us to commit greater sins.

If we pray, fixing our eyes on Him with a sincere heart, there are no prayers that will not be answered. There are no reasons not to pray for long hours. If we pray that way, we will be filled with God's grace. Then we will be able to pray patiently. In trusting God who will surely give the answer, we are able to pray patiently.

George Muller in his autobiography expressed the principle of earnest prayer like this. "It is not enough to start a prayer or to pray rightly. Either how many hours you prayed is not enough. Prayer must be continued with endurance and faith until it is answered."

How about Elijah? There was no rain for three and half years in Israel due to his prayer. However, when he prayed for rain again, he prayed persistently seven times until he saw a small spot of cloud form in the sky, and at last, his prayer was answered.

Hannah's case was similar as well. While she was praying, wailing, and crying, her worries disappeared and faith began to grow. Her worrisome face changed to joy and peace.

Like this, great men and women of faith pray persistently until they see some sign of the answer. When we pray having God at the center of our hearts and making a vow, and when we pray passionately with pure motives, God always hears those prayers and answers our prayers, especially when we pray in tears.

Prayer Calls Greater Faith

While I was serving at the newly planted church, God taught me that the key to victory in ministry was prayer. He taught me the lesson that when we move forward with faith such as, "If we pray, the Lord will answer everything," He will see such faith as good.

Since I was a child, I experienced the Lord's great grace in prayer. As time went by, such great grace increased even more and never decreased. Whenever I prayed to the Lord, he answered most of my prayers. Prayer was truly like a treasure to receive God's grace.

God also let me know that a life of such prayer was the secret to the successful life of a believer. As we pray, faith, the bigger faith, takes place. In fact, the more important thing than having answered prayers to the people of prayer is that they receive even greater faith through prayer. Praying people have a certain faith towards unanswered prayers, living with conviction as if the prayers have already been answered without any proof. It may be the greatest grace of prayer.

When I was in middle school, I suffered from very severe empyema. The symptoms grew worse and my mother was very worried so she took me to Severance Hospital.[10] The doctor blamed my mother with a surprised face.

"How can you allow your child to reach this point?"

The doctor also added that I needed surgery as soon as possible. How would she have felt after hearing this? I cannot even imagine what was going through her mind as we were returning home without the surgery because we could not afford the operation.

Somehow, I needed to get treatment for empyema immediately. Empyema not only hindered my breathing, but it also caused severe headaches, making it difficult

---

[10] Severance Hospital is one of the best hospitals in Seoul, Korea, established in 1885 by Dr. N.H. Allen. It was the first Westernized hospital in Korea.

to concentrate on my studies. I had only God to rely on. So I started to cling onto God in prayer. "Heavenly Father, please heal the empyema. I have no one to rely on but you. Heavenly Father, you know that too well."

Being distressed and being in pain, I wept greatly as I was praying. Then I thought that I needed to see my pastor for help.

I went to see my pastor and gallantly asked for a favor. I asked him to introduce me to a Christian Hospital or other hospitals run by missionaries so I could have a free surgery for my empyema. But to my surprise, he rather yelled at me.

"You have been praying day and night. What kinds of prayer have you prayed?"

The rebuke implanted me an unyielding spirit of prayer. I thought, "He is right." But at the same time, I became very angry. I know it was a childlike mindset, but I thought, "If God does not answer someone like me, who would pray? God is not fair." Then I made a decision.

"I am going to pray over the empyema for the next three days. After that I will never pray for this matter any longer."

After that incident, whenever someone asked me, I said, "I'm okay now." Even though I was still in severe pain, I declared I was healed through prayer.

Surprisingly as time went by, I felt like I was still in pain but sometimes felt fine. In continuing to declare I had been healed by prayer, the pain gradually disappeared. Just to be sure, I went to a hospital again for a checkup. The doctor said that he could not even find any trace of empyema. Ever since then, I have never suffered from it again.

God is alive. God is omniscient and omnipotent. God is faithful.

We must ask God all things with prayer. That is the secret to overcome the world as we live. If you are not happy, even though you believe in the Lord, then it is because you are not asking with an intact faith. You must pray enough until you get some sign of an answer. Those who pray this way will surely be blessed. If you receive the blessing, then you have the faith. When faith grows, joy and peace will overflow. At that time, we finally become joyful Christians.

Prayer Overcomes Circumstances

Around the time when I was getting ready to graduate from seminary, I began to think more seriously about my future. Even though I received God's precious grace greatly, serving at the newly planted church, I thought it would be more helpful to serve in a church already established as an associate pastor for my lifetime pastoral ministry.

"If I continue to serve as a pastor independently, I could fall in a self-frame with a narrow mind and narrow perspective like 'a frog in a well.'"

So I resigned from the church and passed the baton to another pastor. I moved on to serve as a *Jeondosa* (an intern minister before ordination) at Shinhyun Church (the senior pastor was Rev. Suk-Hong Jung). The church was located near the main gate of Ehwa Woman's University. It was before I took the pastor's examination, so I was only able to serve *Jeondosa,* an intern minister.

A day before I was supposed to begin the ministry, I heard news that the invitation was rejected by the session meeting. If I went to the church as a full-time

Jeondosa, I would receive a parsonage and a little salary, but I was told that it was all cancelled.

I guess that the session was not able to entrust the person who had just graduated from seminary as a full-time intern minister. Instead, they wanted to give me a position as a part-time minister in the education department first, and then later, they wanted to entrust me to a full-time intern minister if I was qualified.

My heart was not uncomfortable, and I did not complain about it at all. Instead, I was able to confirm myself on what I really wished to do in my life.

It was not because of salary or better treatment that I decided to walk the way of a servant of the Lord. From the beginning, I chose this way because I wanted to work at any place wherever I would be needed. It did not matter whether I worked as a part-time education minister or full-time associate pastor because it was my wish to live only for the Lord. The only reason I wanted to be an associate pastor was to be a better tool for the Lord. If I considered better treatment, I would not have resigned my ministry at the previous church. So I told the senior pastor, "Pastor, I am okay with the decision. My only desire is to work like an ox for the church. Please let me work as much as I can."

It was not that I did not want to serve as one of the education ministers. What I really did not want was to work occasionally as a part-time minister. I really wanted to work like an ox as much as I could for the Lord. That was what I had been dreaming of since graduating from the seminary.

The next day was Sunday. I woke up early and went to the church hastily. First, I wanted to check out the current situation of the youth department, junior high and high school students' group, where I was placed in charge. Since sincerity and faithfulness of the teachers are most important, I checked the situation in the worship of youth group and preparedness of the teachers for their Sunday school classes without identifying myself to them. There were approximately sixty students at the worship service. It was a relatively small attendance compared to the size of the church. The teachers' preparation for Sunday school classes was very poor, and the attention level of the students during the Bible studies was very digressive. I started to write all these situations down in my pocket book.

During the announcement time in the main service, the senior pastor introduced me as the new intern minister in charge of youth ministry. Upon hearing the announcement, the teachers nodded their heads. Perhaps they were thinking, "Ah, that's why that person was walking around the church early in the morning."

On that Sunday evening service, I delivered my first sermon. As soon as I finished my sermon, the senior pastor suddenly made an announcement.

"Starting tomorrow, we are going to have a revival rally for a week. The speaker is *Jeondosa,* the Intern Minister, Pildo Joung."

What a bolt out of the blue this was! The senior pastor gave an impromptu announcement without dropping any kind of hint to me in advance. I had never led a revival rally before, so how could I lead it now? Moreover, for a week! What a surprising thing it was! It looked like a great "initiation ceremony." It looked like a signal for how much I could work like an ox in the future.

Genuine Revival Begins with Revival of Prayer

After the Sunday evening service, I asked the elder, the head of the youth department, to gather the teachers for a meeting. I mentioned the lack of preparation for

Bible study in the meeting. Sharing my vision and dream for the youth group, in order to fulfill them, I emphasized that the revival of our spirit should take place in our prayer first. I made an announcement that all teachers were to come to church thirty minutes prior to the youth worship service, and I would teach them the key points for the Bible study that day.

Thankfully, the teachers came thirty minutes early and prayed passionately in preparation for the youth worship. Even though I only taught them the key points for the Bible classes briefly, the teachers nodded and highlighted important parts.

The teachers prayed with their students for one hour after Sunday and Wednesday evening worship. Once someone starts praying, the Holy Spirit works together with that person. Only when the Holy Spirit works are the souls of the students changed. It is only the Holy Spirit who changes students to live the Lord-centered, Word-centered, and worship-centered life. If the Holy Spirit meets students personally in their prayers, their lives surely will be changed and dedicated before the Lord.

Indeed, the students started to change. The number of students grew from about 60 students to more than 200 students within three months. That year, the seniors in high school achieved the best results for the university qualification exam in the history of the church. God opened the door widely for the praying students. God had shown us that the key to the revival of even Sunday school was found in prayer as well.

Prayer Brings the Grace of Happiness

The joy of associate pastors comes when they work not passively but actively. For the pastor who sees how the wind blows and tries to act according to the senior pastor's liking, there is no sense of accomplishment and realization such as, "Ah, this is how the Lord's work must be done!"

Regarding this, I was happy when I was serving as an associate pastor. At that time, the senior pastor was very busy from serving actively as a keynote speaker for revival rallies. So he was away from the church often. He trusted me in spite of my shortcomings and gave me opportunities to work as freely as I could. He trusted me in such a way, saying that I did not even have to report to him regarding my ministries.

I started as a part-time intern minister in charge of youth ministry, but soon I became a full-time associate pastor, leading early morning worship and Wednesday worship, visiting the members' homes, and leading even the whole education ministry of the 500 attendance-size church. I served happily and freely as if I was doing the cooperation pastoral ministry with the senior pastor. It was possible because of the senior pastor, Suk-Hong Jung's broad-mindedness and large-scale thinking. Thanks to him, I was able to have great experiences in pastoral ministry for three years.

At that time, I made every effort to fill the empty place of the senior pastor. When I began home visitations, it was five years after the senior pastor came to the church. I kept statistical records on my senior pastor's sermons and hymns often used for five years. The statistics showed me that he preached usually from the New Testament. So I decided to preach at home visitation from the text of the Bible that he did not preach. The statistics were not only about sermons. I also made several graphs regarding how our church had grown in the last five years including church members and even offerings. I constructed those overall statistics and put them up on the wall of the church office. The pastor

106

seemed not to mind when he saw the graphs. He probably thought that this young minister was working hard for the church.

After I made the statistics, I started "the home visitation with words" for each church member, mainly preaching from the Old Testament passages. Even though I was a young and inexperienced minister, the female minister always encouraged me: "I have never experienced a home visitation ministry that was so graceful."

She also mentioned that whenever she had home visitations in the past, she was very uncomfortable because there had been quarrels with the previous associate pastors. But she often asked me to visit more families: "Minister, can we visit only one more member's home? I like this home visitation ministry so much."

A similar situation happened when I was serving at the newly planted church. "The grace of happiness" was poured out in the field of the pastoral ministry.

In fact, I rarely had a bad feeling with female ministers while I was serving with them. While visiting the members' homes together, I served them like my elder sister or my mother because they were much older than me. They also served very well with me for the home visitation with gratitude. Even their level of commitment was no less than male pastors. When the church was working for the construction of a new church building or starting a new, difficult ministry, the female servants exceeded male servants in the commitment of giving their time, finances, and dedication. In some sense, I felt that this was the nature of women. Once they experienced God's grace, it was women who were more passionately devoted to the Lord than men.

Due to these experiences, I have always encouraged my associate pastors to serve their female ministers with good manners even if they are just one year older than they are. I believe that when the field of the pastoral ministry in working together is overflowed by serving, grace, harmony, and gratitude, it is then possible to work the greater pastoral ministry. If an associate pastor is always quarreling with a female minister while working together, it is impossible to love and serve for many sheep in the pastoral ministry.

My time at Shinhyun Church was a time when I worked like an ox. On the other hand, it was also a time that I was free as a bird. My heart was not tied to any hindrance in the ministry. I just served as best as I could, and the rest of it was led by the Holy Spirit of the Lord. It was also possible because I served under such a great senior pastor.

Reflecting on my experience at Shinhyun Church, I often encouraged my associate pastors on the following three aspects of the field of pastoral ministry. The first is the attitude to do your best wholeheartedly and work like an ox in whatever you do: "Be diligent in these matters; give yourself wholly to them, so that everyone may see your progress" (1Timothy 4:15).

Whether it is pastoral ministry or business, on the ground of growth, there is a common attitude so-called "the whole-hearted devotion." If a man insists that he is doing the Lord's work, but has no zeal for the work, it is a sign that he is not ready even for the basic things of the faith. Zeal for the Lord is a basic qualification that every Christian must possess. It is not something to boast about. Therefore, there is no hope for those who do not have zeal for the Lord, and there is no possibility of great growth. Whether it is preparing a sermon, doing home visitations, leading small group meetings, or leading prayer meetings, those who do it with great zeal for the Lord inevitably grow. Those who are committed wholeheartedly will grow quickly to that extent. I have often told my associate pastor the following: "Do not be afraid of making a mistake. I will cover your mistakes and failures. Do not worry about them, but just do the ministry faithfully and passionately. That is the way to grow fast as a pastor. Do anything for the Lord except falling in heresy or cult and committing a sin. Work wholeheartedly and freely without worrying about failure."

I long to meet pastors who do not waste their time and energy on trying to read the senior pastor's face, but who are dedicated to serving passionately and freely as if they are the senior pastor. This is the reason why I told my associate pastors that they did not have to report to me, just like Rev. Suk-Hong Jung told me in the past. I do not interfere with their time and ministry.

Maybe partly due to that, some of the intern ministers in our church have taken dozens of teachers to a mountain for all-night prayers on holidays. They did not even report to me about it. Some of them urge their teachers to come to church on Saturday and have a teacher's prayer meeting.

Doing the ministry wholeheartedly also means "studying thoroughly." From my childhood to the associate pastor days and until now, I have listened to and analyzed sermons of many famous preachers and pastors. It was because I felt deeply that I still have a lot of room to grow; therefore, I could not avoid listening to their sermons. Sometimes, I only slept about two hours, as I analyzed the data I collected in the meetings in which I participated. Sometimes I carried a tape recorder to record sermons. When I was young, I bought more than 100 sermon tapes of a pastor and listened to all of them. My room was full with analytical papers on how each pastor interpreted and preached each text in the Bible. Also, my room was full with sermons that I analyzed according to the texts from Genesis 1 to Revelations 22. If my sermon was from Genesis 13, the basic step for my sermon preparation was to take out all the sermons on Genesis 13 and study them. Serving wholeheartedly for pastors also means having enough time to mediate, study the Bible and to pray. If a pastor spends most of his time on other visible things, that pastor will burn out inevitably. The overflowing grace will disappear.

Now I am approaching the age of seventy. Very often, I tell my associate pastors that I need to learn from them because I am outdated. The data that I have collected, the materials that I studied, and the things that I knew are from the past, so I encourage all my associate pastors to exceed me in every way so that they can actively serve in every aspect of their ministry. In fact, I learned and received much help from my associate pastors. They were sometimes better than me even in using an illustration for preaching.

The period as an associate pastor is a time to accumulate enough ministerial resources while serving like an ox. Even for a very competent associate pastor, while he is preaching from early morning worship to Sunday preaching, his resources usually run out within three months when he starts to serve as a senior pastor of a larger church. Although he has maintained good relationships with the members of the church during his associate pastor days, once he becomes a senior pastor, very often he faces many relationship problems with other members of the new church. Often, it is because he does not know how to handle the full weight and spiritual responsibilities coming from this position.

God's servants are playing a role like prophets in the Old Testament. They have a calling to oversee the life of the members through the Word of God and guide them onto the right path. This is why I began to write a "Pastoral Manual" ever since I was in seminary. When a problem occurred in the church, I wrote why the problems arose, how it was resolved, and whether the resolution method was the best way or not. One day, I had an extraordinary dream. Writing things about what happened after the dream and how I understood the meaning of the dream in this situation, I sought wisdom from God. I also wrote in detail like "when there was a misunderstanding, I just kept silent and prayed instead of trying to explain, and then these results came out." I prepared myself to be a senior pastor like this for a long time.

These records were very helpful to me because they contained many principles of the pastoral ministry. When a similar situation happens, it is very applicable in determining how to find a resolution. Whatever we do for the Lord's work, if we do our best wholeheartedly, God gives us wisdom. When we learn diligently and apply genuinely, "a pastoral manual for my ministry" comes out.

The second basic aspect that must be in the field of pastoral ministry is "Grace." Aside from the wholehearted devotion, there must be grace. With only our enthusiasm, we cannot make our ministry grow. Whether you are doing a home visitation, delivering a sermon, or leading a prayer meeting, there has to be grace. If there is grace within the church, church members will voluntarily come to church no matter how far they live. If there is no grace, no matter how close they live to the church and how often their pastor shouts persuasively to come to prayer meeting, there are only a few members that will show up. Therefore, the best compliment to a pastor is, "Our pastor is a man of grace." If there are only few members coming to the prayer meeting, the pastor must lead the prayer meeting more in grace. For this, the pastor himself must live in grace. If possible, pastors should live as a lump of grace. Even as people see his face, they should feel the grace. Even if he says a word, still people should feel the grace. To be such a pastor like Jesus must be our eternal hope and goal.

Even if you are filled with zeal and grace, there is one more thing that must not be missing. It is love. Love is the very first and the most important fruit of the Holy Spirit, and it is the ultimate goal in the field of the pastoral ministry. After all, human beings naturally like those people who love themselves. When they are convinced that you love them and even their souls, they will follow your guidance and obey your words. Thus, pastors who are doing their ministry successfully always give a clear conviction to their congregation like, "I love you so much!" Therefore, whenever they just think about their pastor, they think, "Oh, my pastor likes me and loves me so much!" When there is this kind of love, the souls are moved.

When a sermon is delivered in the language of love, the members will respond in "Amen" to the messages. When a pastor is filled with love, the love will also be filled in the sermons that he is giving and on his face as well. In the same manner, when a pastor has anger in his heart, it appears within his sermon and on his face as well.

Looking at these three basic elements, pastors have to be people who constantly examine themselves. When troubles or hardships come to the field of pastoral ministry, pastors should know how to examine themselves first. Satan is always aiming at pastors to destroy the church. Therefore, pastors must reflect on themselves before God, and they must have holiness, knowing how to figure out the reasons of the problems within their heart. Pastors should always ask themselves, "Do I need more love? Do I need more grace? Do I need more zeal for God?" As much as I love, and as much as I receive grace, the field of pastoral ministry is surely filled with love and grace.

I am not sure how faithful I was to these principles while I served at Shinhyun Church for three years. However, even when I was not able to be faithful to these principles, the Lord poured out abundant grace on me and led me closely. In my time at the church, God taught me and told me through His still voice what kind of heart a pastor must have and what church members really need. God has always been leading me as my shepherd.

CHAPTER 5

Church Planting: With Obedience From The First Button

The Pastor's Mind Has to Burn with the Love of Jesus

The Shinhyun Church is unforgettable as the place where I met my beloved wife. Since I was never interested in getting married, I was in total shock when I heard that I could not be ordained if I was single. So, I started to search for my bride in a hurry. However, just at the right moment, God sent the best bride that He had prepared for me. God allowed me a godly female servant as my wife, who was raised with education and instruction of the Lord in the family of an elder.

As I mentioned earlier, right after the marriage, I served as a chaplain in the Air Force for three years. During those years, God taught me that He is all sovereign in pastoral ministry. No matter how great the desire of our hearts, we will never outdo God's heart.

God's love toward a soul is so great to the point He would rather exchange the entire world for that soul. His love is so passionate that He sent His one and only Son into the world and had Him crucified on the cross. Therefore, God wants to do his salvation work sovereignly. I realized that fact when I was working as a chaplain. God is just looking for a man who is after His own heart. He is looking for the vessel, a clean vessel that the Holy Spirit can use as His tool. But if the vessel becomes stained, idle against the purpose of the owner, haughty before his Lord, or tries to steal God's glory, then the vessel cannot be used any longer.

During my chaplaincy, God instructed me directly and taught me His precious will. I saw the passion and will of God to save souls of all the military personnel in the corps. I now had the firm faith that the Holy Spirit would carry out everything anytime as long as He grasps us completely. In a sense, because I was so weak, I rather think He had cherished and led me more.

"He brought his people out like a flock; he led them like sheep through the desert" (Psalms 78:52).

About the time when I was discharged from military service, I had many plans thinking I would do pastoral ministry in Seoul. I was trying to work immediately for any church in Seoul, if the church would invite me. I never imagined ministering outside of Seoul because aside from serving as chaplain in the Air Force, I never once left the city.

But just before the discharge, I was faced with a problem. Five different offers came all at once from Seoul. If there were a calling from only one church, I would have gone to that church without any doubt. But since I received offers from five different churches simultaneously, I couldn't figure out the will of God. I couldn't help but pray.

"Please, tell me where I must go. I'm afraid that if I make a decision, it could be a selfish decision. I don't want to decide based on my knowledge. So, Father, please tell me. I just want to obey your will."

Being pressed, I prayed finally, "Then, I will go to the church where someone approaches me first. I will go without reserve accepting it is as your will."

After the prayer, much to my surprise, someone came to visit me immediately. However, that person was not from Seoul, but from Busan, asking me to plant a church in that city. He was sent by Elder Hae-Chan Jung from Choryang Church. Elder Hae-Chan Jung, the third son of the Elder Tae-Sung Jung, was a businessman who made a vow to God in prayer: "If this problem is solved, I will build a church and dedicate it to God." When he received the answer from the Lord, he was looking for a pastor who would work for planting a church in order to keep his vow to the Lord.

I could not say anything because it was a totally unexpected visit. I never expected something like this to happen. I asked him to give me a week. I told him that I would pray and decide after I prayed. When I was working as a minister after seminary, I had already experienced how difficult it was to plant a church. Although I had experienced it through difficult situations, God poured out greater grace, but I was not ready to step up again voluntarily for church planting. Only those who are working for planting a church know how difficult the ministry of church planting is. When there is no help, it is impossible to describe the hardships and pains for the ministry of church planting. I was hesitant to take that offer in spite of the elder's promise to build a church. Planting a church was just that difficult. I could not help but pray for the matter. "Lord! I never said that I would plant a church. I said that I would go to a church amongst the five churches in Seoul. Why did you send him to me? What do I need to do?"

I prayed about this issue from Monday to Wednesday, but there was no answer from the Lord. My mind was not shaken following God's silence. However, starting on Thursday, whenever I closed my eyes to pray, I saw thousands of people gathered together in all natural colors. Although I had received much grace in prayer, it was the first time that I saw a vision from the Lord. Whenever I closed my eyes, the same vision appeared. I even heard the Lord's voice: "Where would you go leaving these sheep? Where would you go leaving these sheep?"

Not only was it so mysterious, but also so clear that I could not pray any more. "Oh, Lord. I will obey you. I will accept this sign as God's call to plant a church."

That was the beginning of Sooyoungro Church. By that time, I did not have a name for the church, and a place for worship was not decided as well. However, through the vision and the voice of the Lord, I could feel God's fervent love toward the church that was about to be planted.

The Lord who loves Busan greatly wanted to begin His great work through Sooyoungro Church. I did not know the flocks that He showed me, yet in the presence of the Lord's heart to love them so much, my heart was burning as well. "The Lord must have a purpose; therefore, he moved the Elder's heart, hindered me from going to Seoul and showed me the vision. Then, I have nothing to fear. The Lord will take care of everything. After all, He will lead us, who are used as His tools, to the best way."

As I responded to God's call in obedience, the Lord poured out the great dream and vision for the church in my heart. Fears disappeared, and so did worries and anxieties. It all happened in a moment. As soon as I responded, "Yes, I will follow you" the assurance that the Lord would take care of everything grabbed me. My heart was filled with the expectations for the works that God would do through the newly planted church.

God Will Do His Work

At that time, Elder Jung was still serving at Choryang Church, so he promised his financial and prayer support for the new church and returned to his home church to serve. He had entrusted everything to me. In that sense, I was a pastor who was specially treated.

From the beginning, he had constructed the church building, brought two faithful families of deacons to assist my ministry, and paid my salary for a year. Looking back, I have nothing to boast about regarding the process that Sooyoungro Church was established and grown. Probably, everyone can do pastoral ministry successfully under such great conditions for church planting.

From the beginning, therefore, I had great faith that God would do all things for the church since God the Father founded this church, not I. In addition, I was so sure that God would lead me to the best way this time as well, as God the Father has always been good to me by giving me the best. Whenever you start something, it is very important to begin with such a faith.

As I was looking around for the location of the church, I was filled with the faith. "God will provide the best land that will be used to save countless souls."

I had grown up praying with countless prayers over financial matters and money-related worries, but God had set me free from worries and anxieties about financial matters at some point. He always provided me with more than what I asked for. In that sense, how useless it is to worry. After all, God will feed, clothe, and provide in the best way. When looking for the church location, I only prayed for the wisdom to discern "the best land that God allows." Surely God provides the best land of great value.

The area around the Sooyoung Rotary, one of the greatest places where many people would gather, was waiting for us. It was the time when America was defeated in the Vietnam War, so the atmosphere of Korea was very unstable as well. The tendency not to own land, but to possess cash in order to manage some emergency situation was prevalent. Naturally, the price of the land began to drop incessantly. Thanks to that milieu, we could purchase land of great value easily.

After deciding to establish the church building on the land, I just had to pray. Having no one to pray with me, I began to pray all night alone, sitting on a veneer board in the front yard of the sanctuary site. On the front yard of the construction, because I had to defeat Satan's attack, I prayed all night with a determination to repulse the attack of Satan and win a victory.

> Up, and fight against the devil, You whose sins are washed away!
> Jesus Christ is waiting, open armed.
> For all who trust and pray. He is eager to assist you;
> Come to Him and don't delay. Come now, His call is clear!
> Glory glory, hallelujah! Glory glory, hallelujah!
> Glory glory, hallelujah! For triumph drawing near!
> (Korean Hymnal 388, 3rd stanza)

When I was praying all night, there were endless distractions that came to my attention. Unusual rattling noises, the sound of the wind, and the sound of something being dragged to and fro. It looked as if Satan's struggling to stop my prayer seemed to reach its extremes. But nothing could stop the prayer toward God and His works. Once I was equipped by the prayer, everything went smoothly with great speed. There were voices from residents in that area protesting against construction of the church, when in reality, nobody acted on it, and the voices to protest soon disappeared.

Finally, on December 14, 1975, Sooyoungro Church glorified God by having its first worship service. Since the building construction was not completely finished yet, we had the worship services in the elementary school Bible study room. With two families of deacons, a female evangelist who was one of the distant relatives of Elder Jung, and my family present, Sooyoungro Church started in this way. As a newly planted church, it was a solid start.

The First Principle of Shepherding in Church Planting: Obey to the End

The ministry at Sooyoungro Church has been filled by the help of the Holy Spirit every step of the way. Because the church was located in the middle of the rotary, there were many people visiting the church as they were passing by here and there. God sent such a big number of people who were praying an "all night prayer," and ever since we started the church, the fire of the prayer has never gone out. Even some people who were not members of our church came to pray for us through the night. Although I have never been eloquent in speech and less qualified on pastoral ministry, we were always busy on Sundays welcoming new-comers. We had newcomers sign up for membership every Sunday, so the number of members increased to two hundred in one year. Whatever we prayed, it seemed all of our prayers were being answered. All of our needs were filled immediately.

Watching over this kind of growth, even I was sur-prised. Of course, we have to pray very persistently and be faithful to the Lord all the time; however, although we do our best in doing so, the revival does not happen just because of that. Then, how were all these things even possible? God only told me to stay in Busan, and God only told me to plant a church as well; therefore I did. That's all. But God has been pouring out overflowing blessings.

At that time, I realized the promise of God's Word being fulfilled. "All these blessings will come upon you and accompany you if you obey the Lord your God" (Deuteronomy 28:2). If we only obey to do His will, it is God's heart to give and entrust everything to us. Since the Lord is pleased to bless us, He is waiting sincerely for us only to obey Him.

If I were to give a reason why Jesus chose his dis-ciples and made them apostles, even though they had many shortcomings and mistakes, it was due to their obedience. When the Lord said, "Follow me," they fol-lowed the Lord, leaving their boats and nets. It was unconditional obedience. Their capability and academic level was not important to Jesus. He only saw their obe-dience. Yes, the work of the Lord begins with obedience. When Jesus was resurrected and taken up to heaven, what were His last words?

"Do not leave Jerusalem, but wait for the gift my Father promised, which you have heard me speak about" (Acts 1:4).

The Lord requires obedience. More than 500 people heard this word of the Lord. However, most of them merely listened but did not obey. Many people had left for several reasons, and only 120 disciples remained to wait for the promised Holy Spirit. Those who obeyed were filled with the Holy Spirit. It is important that as you obey, obey until the end.

I understand this fact when I preach. When I preach even the same sermon, most people just listen, and only a few obey. Many people just listen to the Word, then forget and live in their own way, which is dead faith. Listening to the Word and acting on it is obedience. When you listen to the Word, believe and trust the Word just as it is and obey with conviction that the work of the Lord has begun, this is a true faith and a true belief.

When you obey in this manner, you will be blessed in many ways. The first blessing is that you receive God's love.

"Whoever has my commands and keeps them is the one who loves me. The one who loves me will be loved by my Father, and I too will love them and show myself to them" (John 14:21).

You just need to believe in this word as it is. If you are obedient to God, God the Father, Jesus the Lord, and the Holy Spirit will love you. By obeying God, you can cultivate an intimate relationship with the Triune God.

The second blessing is to those who obey God, and it is the opening of their spiritual eyes. Read carefully the last part of John 14:21: "I too will love them and show myself to them" (John 14:21).

He said He would show Himself to those who obey. Read this verse again comparing it with the next one.

"The Lord continued to appear at Shiloh . . . He revealed himself to Samuel through his word" (1 Samuel 3:21).

"The visions of the Lord" were not so common during the times when Eli was a priest. At that time, the world was so depraved morally and darkened spiritually that nobody could hear God's voice or see a vision. There was no prophet during this time. But Samuel heard God's voice from his childhood. What God said to Samuel concerning the house of Eli the priest came true. God's promise to Samuel, that his words would never fall to the ground, was completely fulfilled. Seeing these fulfillments, the Israelites recognized that Samuel was a true prophet of the Lord.

When we have to decide on an important issue in our pastoral ministry, a time must come where we are seeking God's presence as He had shown Himself in the Book of Acts. It is because there are times when we are inevitably faced with problems that cannot be resolved with human wisdom or might. If God speaks just one word, and if the Lord resolves the problems, we know that all the problems will be resolved at once. We want to hear his voice, even just one word.

At this moment, there is one thing God wants, and it is obedience. God speaks to those who live and obey, no matter what He says. God speaks clearly to those who are willing to obey unconditionally without any reason. Like Abraham, when he was told to "sacrifice your only son," to those who can give unconditionally, the Lord speaks pleasantly. God opens and shows a deep spiritual world to those who obey.

Sometimes pastors from my denomination see me with suspicious eyes when I am giving my testimony. "How on earth do you hear God's voice? Do you hear it audibly?"

Then I have no way of explaining that. "You'll know when you hear it."

When Saul met the resurrected Jesus on his way to Damascus and heard His voice, other people who were with him could not hear the voice as well. That is the voice of God. Even if we are in the same place, it is the voice of God that some can hear and others cannot. Most of the people fail to hear God's voice. There is a reason for this.

Disobedient people cannot hear the voice of God. To those, it is the same whether they hear the voice of God or not. To the person who only listens, but does not obey, why will He speak? God knows everything, even the inner heart. He even knows whether we will obey or not when we hear His voice. That's why sometimes He rebukes, sometimes asks, and sometimes commands as He leads us. What matters the most is whether we obey when we realize God's will. As long as we just obey God's will, our obedience will return to us as a fruit of joy. This is why I get excited to hear God's voice, even when it is a voice of rebuking.

The biggest reason why most people fail to obey is because of greed. When you are blinded by greed, you cannot obey. When you become greedy, your discernment gets clouded, your mind gets filled with worries, and you become sickly tired from all the stress. However, your heart will be flooded with peace once you overcome a greedy heart. Worries disappear, and your mind finds simplicity. No matter what the Lord says, you can respond in unconditional obedience. You can see a much deeper level of the spiritual world.

This is not to say that you should live seeking mystical experiences. The Lord performs wonders and miracles, but Satan also can do wonders and give us false signs. Therefore, if we want to reach the deepest spiritual level, we must be faithful to the Bible, the Word of God. The Word itself is the revelation, and the Word itself is the voice of God. Therefore, if we are living in obedience thoroughly, we can live a life being led by the Holy Spirit. Sometimes we can hear the voice of God clearly. Sometimes while meditating on God's Word, the Word comes in my heart penetrating even to dividing joints and marrow, and sometimes the Word becomes a light for my path. Therefore, those who obey the Word can enter into a deeper spiritual world.

The third blessing of those who obey is "the blessing of Immanuel."

"Jesus replied, 'Anyone who loves me will obey my teaching. My Father will love them, and we will come to them and make our home with him'" (John 14:23).

What a blessed word! It is the promise of the Holy Father, the Holy Son, and the Holy Spirit to be with me completely. The blessing of Immanuel to live with God comes to me. If God is with me, what can obstruct me? The blessing of Immanuel is the blessing of blessings and the joy of joys.

Therefore, this should be our foremost prayer theme: "Please, help me live in obedience. Help me to live a life obeying only your will!"

Why do we need to pray like this? It is because if something is done by God's will, it is the best way, and anything that belongs to God is the best no matter what it is. God's thoughts are the best thoughts, God's plans are the best plans, God's ways are the best ways, and the results of God's doing are the best results. After all, for something to be done by God's will is the best way. If we have a clear conviction on that, we cannot help but pray this way all day and all night.

"God, my wish is to live according to your perfect will. Please teach me what your will is."

If we live in God's will even if it is the way of the cross, the way will lead me into the happiest, the most

125

blessed, and the most successful life that I could ever have. This is the principle of God's kingdom.

Jesus, who knew this principle, prayed like this before taking up the cross: ". . . Yet not my will, but yours be done" (Luke 22:42).

This prayer of Jesus is the greatest prayer in history. It is the model prayer we should follow. Living in God's will never end in the pain of the cross, but gives us the blessed and glorious life with the crown of glory. It is the path where the blessing of Jehovah Jirah will be poured out.

The Second Principle of Shepherding in Church Planting: Do Not Depend on People and Their Background

One of the most difficult things while planting a church was there were no co-workers. If anyone comes to the new church, then the pastor can do anything. However, there is nothing more discouraging and heart-breaking for pastors than when they see no people joining the church after it has been planted for several months. This is why pastors usually involve some of their relatives or close acquaintances when planting a new church.

However, this can be difficult over time when a pastor starts the ministry bringing in relatives and friends. In some cases, this can become a pitfall to the ministry. No one is perfect, but when a pastor starts the ministry with those of blood ties and regional relation, eventually they often try to manipulate the pastor because they know of the pastor's weak points and mistakes.

A pastor I know was looking for someone who would help him when he started planting a church. One day, he incidentally met an elder who had gone to the same high school with him. The pastor pleaded with him. "Hey! Please help me. Who else will help me if you don't?" However, after bringing this elder who was serving faithfully in another church, strange happenings started to arise within the church. Members of the church often saw the communication between the pastor and elder, informally greeting each other, saying "Hey!" At first, it seemed that the co-work with the elder was very helpful for establishing the church. He was a big help in financial matters and drawing people to church, but as the church grew to a certain size, problems began to arise. During the vestry meetings (office-holders' meetings) of the church, the elder often addressed the pastor in an indecent manner.

"Hey, I don't think it's going to work." "Okay, then, you are the pastor, so you do it." So the pastor's authority and face fell to the ground.[11]

No matter how young the pastor, there are reasons why deacons and elders use respectful language when they address him. Through the use of respectful language, they indicate their willingness to "obey the leadership of the pastor who has been anointed as the servant of the Lord" and to recognize and respect his authority. Authority is very important. The apostle Paul, therefore, exhorted Timothy "do not let anyone look down on you because you are young."

In that sense, I think it is the grace of God that I planted a church not in Seoul but in Busan. Didn't the Scripture say that only in his hometown is a prophet without honor? Even now sometimes when I meet my

---

[11] In Korean Christian culture, pastors are well respected. So when he is addressed, it is important to use proper, respectful language, but the elder addressed the pastor like a school friend. That is not edifying the pastor in front of the congregation.

alumni friends in Seoul, there are many friends who call out to me, "Hey, Pildo." Of course, it is no problem at all. However, it is impossible to even imagine in our church. In our church, no matter how young the pastor is, the elders, who are about the age of the pastor's father, speak to the pastor in respectful words to obey and follow him. So I sometimes laugh to myself and say, "My church would not have grown as much as it has if I had planted a church in Seoul. It was possible because my faults and mistakes had been concealed in Busan."

In fact, pastors often are tempted to bring in their relatives or friends in regional relations no matter what it costs because they need even one person when they first plant a church. But even in that case, we need to wait for the souls that God would send, putting our hope in God. This is the faith looking toward God alone.

If a pastor does his pastoral ministry bringing in his relatives or wealthy friends, the pastor is likely to depend on those people rather than on God whenever he is faced with difficulty in his ministry. He feels that he cannot do his ministry, even if those people are not there. In doing so, he relies on them more than God at some point, and eventually he serves men as his idol. Idol worship should not be any particular thing. If one relies on human beings, it is idol worship. At that time, a demon begins to work.

When a demon starts to work, the good co-worker of yesterday all of a sudden turns into a rod to beat down the pastor. Especially in newly planted churches that depend on relatives or friends from the same regional area, the pastoral ministry can fall into many difficulties. In this situation, there is a certain tendency that occurs. That is, those people who are from the same region as the pastor appear as the important persons in the church. In these churches, there is no room for those from different regions. If a member from a different region can settle in the church, the church is not shown positively as a strong church compared to those in the area. There are continuous divisions and quarrels in those churches.

So our church has determined from the beginning not to discriminate people according to their regional backgrounds. I did not select my associate pastors based on the region itself, whether they were from Youngnam Province (a southeast region in Korea), Honam Province (a southwest region in Korea), or Seoul. Though Sooyoungro Church is located in Busan, later I came to realize that the pastors from Jullado (a southwest area in Korea) were so faithful and doing very well in their ministry. I was able to see facts that I would never have been able to see if I had differentiated their background. Since pastors serving at our church are all from different regions of the country, the members of the church are the same as pastors. Regardless of their backgrounds, whether it is Kangwon Province (a Northeast region in Korea), Julla Province, Chungcheong Province (a central region in Korea), Jeju Province or Busan, it is a church where anyone can join us in hands and pray together.

No matter how burdensome it is right now in your ministry, you must not depend on your kinsmen and your father's household. That is a shortcut for the church to grow. Do you have not one person to depend on? If this is your situation, then all the more the pastor has to wait on God with great expectations and wait for the souls that He will send. Sooner or later, God will send a group of the best workers. It is God who guides man's steps.

The Third Principle of Shepherding in Church Planting: A Bad Pastor Is a Bigger Problem than a Bad Member.

In pastoral ministry, an inevitable test is the conflict with the members. I too have had many troubles to pass this test. As I mentioned earlier, a principle of pastoral ministry is that when a flock of sheep comes and joins the church, not only are good sheep coming, but bad sheep are coming at the same time.

At the beginning stage of my ministry, I struggled so much with this problem. I was just pressing onward for the glory of the Lord, but one of the members went around slandering me to everyone. Whenever I heard the stories, I was hurt with heart-breaking pain. If we look at a person with hateful eyes, everything about the person seems to be hateful. Like this, he saw every aspect of me with distortion. He misunderstood my words as having a bad meaning, although I said the same thing, and spread the things he misunderstood out to every one of his own accord.

I also experienced my heart beginning to be filled with hate for this person as time went by. It was a time when there were not many members at church. So I used to pray for my church members, one by one, calling their names, to bless them during my prayer time at dawn. However, when it came to that particular person's turn, my prayer stopped. The hatred toward him in my heart hindered me from sincerely praying for this person.

Additionally, when standing on the pulpit to preach with that enmity in my heart, I could not preach well. God is love. The Word of God, which is love, can never be proclaimed purely if the enmity exists in the heart of the preacher when we try to proclaim the Word of

God in the vessel of enmity, the Word of God delivered is being compromised. In this situation, the Holy Spirit cannot work in full measure. The revival of the church will be stymied as well. Because of just one pastor, the foundation of a church is shaken.

By the Holy Spirit's work to recognize the problem, I realized how serious it was. With determination not to play a tug of hatred anymore, I got down on my knees to pray tenaciously. While praying for each member to bless them, I prayed for him longer than anyone else. Until my heart became a genuine heart to bless him, until the prayer of blessing for him was lifted up completely to God, and until I decided to love him, I prayed continually. At one moment while I was praying, I was convinced that God was pleased to receive that prayer. At that time, I realized that when a hateful heart toward someone is conceived in my heart, if I do not pay back with hatred but embrace the soul and pray, the hatred can be transformed into a heart of love and blessings.

When I prayed and blessed him, the Holy Spirit surely started touching the heart of this person. Is there anyone who will dislike a pastor who prays for him? Gradually, it looked as if the problem was solved.

One day, the Lord helped me realize one lesson unexpectedly through His Word in Numbers in which the prophet Balaam appeared. Summoned by Balak, who was king of Moab to "come and put a curse on the Israelites," Balaam heard an insult from his donkey on his way to Moab with the noblemen of Moab. There is no one in the Bible who is more ridiculous than he is. What a man who was to be rebuked not by man but by a mere donkey! Why on earth did Balaam become such a foolish person? Even his donkey, a mere animal, saw the angel of the Lord and turned away, but Balaam, blinded by his greed, could not see the angel of the Lord standing in the road. In the very moment, he was worse than the donkey.

All of a sudden, God gave me an understanding while I was praying. Am I not a pastor who deserves to be reprimanded by a donkey like Balaam was? In spite of that, since it was a man who blamed me, it was fortunate. So I gave my thanks to God sincerely in my prayer.

"Thank you. Thank you, Lord! I am a sinner who must be rebuked by a donkey. In spite of that, since you led me to be reprimanded not by donkey but by man, I thank you for this."

I testified this story as it was during the following Sunday sermon. After that, something very amazing happened. The person who used to spread rumors and slander me changed to someone who went around respecting, complimenting, and praising me.

On another occasion, I was struggling with a deacon who hindered the growth of the church if I allowed him to be in our church continually. Once again, I started a special prayer time to negotiate before God. Alone in the empty chapel, I cried out. "God my Father, you have to choose either to drive this person out of the church or send me to another church. Tonight choose either to take me or to take that person with you."

It was a dreadful prayer. I cried out all night. But at dawn, all of a sudden, I heard the Lord say to me loudly.

"You're the problem!"

What? I thought the other person was the problem, so I was speechless before the Lord who told me that I was the problem. So like a child, I prayed with tears.

"Father, forgive me. I am the pastor with many faults who doesn't even know my own faults. Forgive me!"

Hearing this prayer, the Lord spoke with a gentle voice.

"It is you that I hold and work with. It is not the deacon. The deacon is a mere sheep entrusted to you. Whether the church grows or not is totally up to you because I am holding you to work with."

As soon as I heard the voice, I prayed.

"Thank you. Thank you. I won't ever complain about the sheep. I will consider every problem of the church my problem."

After that, I did not complain about any member of the church. I even stopped preaching sermons to rebuke any of them. Even if you preach to rebuke the members with problems, they will not listen. Irrelevantly, the good and faithful church members will listen and get hurt. Therefore, it is not beneficial for the growth of the church.

The pastor is the one who speaks on behalf of God. So only after he empties himself completely and fills to the brim with love towards the sheep, can he preach the Word rightly. After realizing this fact, I changed the whole paradigm of my sermon. I never again prepared or preached God's Word to target specific people, as saying, "Listen somebody!" If I particularly recall any church members while preparing my message, I am reminded of the most beloved church members or the most proud church members. I prepared God's Word with a heart to feed the best food to those church members.

As a result, the entire congregation hearing my message had peace on their faces. Many gave me feedback saying that they felt as if "God's Word was touching their hearts deeply." They said they could feel how much I loved them, and they could understand my loving heart toward them. At that time, I realized that if the pastor empties himself and communicates God's Word solely inspired by God, the Holy Spirit will be working in each individual in a way that best suits each one's needs. Those who should repent will repent, those who need to be healed will be healed, and those who need comfort will be comforted by the Holy Spirit. The ministry of preaching God's words requires my whole being to be completely surrendered as a tool of the Holy Spirit. It is the ministry that the Holy Spirit has to be the Lord, not I. When a preacher is preaching, the most important thing to the preacher is the field of his heart. The most important factor to receive God's grace is to ask, "In what state of mind do you preach?" rather than "How well are you preaching?" I believe that the Lord wanted to teach me this truth. It is why, I think, the Lord said, "You're the problem!" I believe He did not want to see me preaching His word out of my hatred and bitterness any longer. He wanted Sooyoungro Church to be overflowing with the Word of grace. I believe that is why He rebuked me.

The Fourth Principle of Shepherding in Church Planting: A Test is a Passage to Grace

In the history of Sooyoungro Church, just like any other church, there were some big and small trials. However, they was nothing but a mere test. The tests could not be a factor to hinder the growth of the church. On the contrary, the tests seemed like a sign that God shows prior to the growth of the church. Although it had been very difficult to resolve the trials when they came, after we went through the trials, there were always gifts God prepared behind them. Therefore, from a certain point, I have a habit of expecting and waiting for what God would do when a trial comes.

At the beginning stage of the church planting, as newcomers flooded into the church, I experienced various experiences through church members all at once. While numerous good and faithful workers came, a number of people with many problems came to the church as well. It looked as if every day brought a series of problems. There was a man who was good at quarrelling that came and caused problems. There was a person with malicious intentions who caused a storm in the church and left. There was a man who nagged me to buy him a house whenever he met me. No matter how hard I tried to persuade him that I could not buy him a house because I did not even have one, it was useless. He rather talked back to me.

"Does it make sense that such a rich church like this can't buy a house for a poor guy like me?"

I'm sure every church and every pastor has times of headaches because of the people.

Out of many, one incident caused by a couple, who were serving deacons left me a surprise with an important lesson. After registering as members of our church, the young couple had been the focus of interests and attention from all of the church members in our congregation. They were so diligent in serving the church. They served in the choir, Sunday school, and even attended dawn prayer meetings every day. They were always kind and tenderhearted to everyone. So everyone in the church spoke well of them. "They are the treasures of our church. Treasures!"

Everyone had lavished compliments of the young couple unanimously, and the couple looked like it was good to deserve such praises by the church members. One day, however, an unexpected incident took place. Even long after the incident, we could not believe the fact that the couple was responsible.

On that day, the couple that had been good and faithful in the church visited the houses of all the church members on a motorcycle. They told the members, "About thousands of million won (around thousands of dollars) will be wired from Seoul tonight, but I have an urgent need for money, so will you lend me some money right now for an hour?"

Several thousands of million won were very large amounts of money at that time. But since they had a very good reputation and earned the trust from church members, everyone gave them as much as they could from one hundred thousand won, one million won or two million won. There was even someone who borrowed money from his neighborhood and handed it right in the hands of the couple.

The couple, however, disappeared with all the money from our church members. They did not show up at the church again. The couple had approached the church from the beginning with the intention to defraud. The whole church was thrown into an uproar. Everyone was speechless and dumbfounded.

These kinds of trials occurred in the church continually. One incident after another took place. As more people came to church at once, more troubles took place at the same time.

In this kind of situation, as the senior pastor, I could not help but pray for the church with a heart to die until I found some kind of solution from the Lord. When there are many church members discouraging the pastor and many incidents occurring in the church, it means there is a serious spiritual battle taking place. What kind of city is Busan? You can see women wearing Buddhist monk's clothes and shopping in the open market. Busan is such a city that the culture of Buddhism and idolatry has been generalized deeply. To win a victory over Satan in such a city, there is no way but to put on the full spiritual armor of God. If you try to solve problems by human power, contrary to your will, you would get caught in the scheme of Satan and lose the battle according to Satan's will. Therefore, the worse the incident becomes, the more the pastor must devote himself to prayer. By meeting with God in prayer, you can experience the problem that looked like a giant mountain disappearing in a split second. When the pastor fails to pray when the problem is growing bigger and bigger, the heart of the pastor then becomes more impatient. If you are in a state of anxiety and desperation, many church problems will come on you like a big wave. It will cause you to lose sleep at night, and eventually it makes pastors try to solve the problem with human ways. The pastor calls for an elders' and deacons' meeting to explain and enforce. The more the pastor struggles to unravel the tangled threads of the problem, the more seriously it will get caught up. In the end, it gets tangled beyond your capacity to free it.

I, too, sometimes made that kind of mistake absurdly. Whenever I faced a problem, how incredibly uncomfortable I was! In the end, my impatience and my human zeal ruined God's work.

On the contrary, when bigger problems came along, the more I fasted, repented, and prayed leaving everything up to God, the more the problem was unexpectedly solved. When I prayed and waited, I could see the Holy Spirit work it out in such a wonderful manner. The problem solver was always the Holy Spirit.

Looking back, it was the Holy Spirit who solved the problem already. I couldn't help but exclaim in wonder whenever I confirmed the fact again and again. Yes, the pastor has to be the one who awaits the Holy Spirit in prayer. If you pray and wait for the Holy Spirit, He will subdue the incident by the Word or by incurring another incident. The person who caused the problem would disappear unnoticed. The stiff-necked person would repent and be changed in God's grace. As the Holy

Spirit is at work in that way, the church will be changed into a greater courtyard of great grace. The ministry can be destroyed in a moment. That is why the pastor must pray all the time. When a trial comes, he must pray to God with a heart that he will die. If you pray, you will receive power; if you receive power, your messages will be changed; and if your message is changed, the congregation will receive the grace of God. Then, the pastor will have nothing to fear even if a test comes, and his church will become filled with the Lord's grace. Because grace is poured out, the church will grow after tests, and the abounding joy will be added to your church after the trials. In some sense, this is the enjoyment of the pastoral ministry. Even the trial becomes a passage to God's grace.

> Light after darkness, Gain after loss, strength after weakness, Crown after cross;
> Sweet after bitter, Hope after fears, Home after wandering, Praise after tears//
> Sheaves after sowing, Sun after rain, Sight after mystery, Peace after pain;
> Joy after sorrow, Calm after blast, Rest after weariness, Sweet rest at last//
> Near after distant, Gleam after gloom, Love after loneliness, Life after tomb
> After long agony, Rapture of bliss, Right was the pathway Leading to this//
> Bliss after agony, Gain after loss, Home after wandering, Crown after cross,
> After breath's failure, Life evermore, Such ways are truth, Blessed and sure!
> (Korean Hymn 535)

CHAPTER 6

Growth: Pride Stops It

The Real Senior Pastor of the Church Is Jesus

When the church had overcome various tests and grown larger in size, as the pastor, my heart was filled with confidence. Is there anything to make the pastor's heart happier than when there is continuous enrollment of newcomers every week and the congregation responding with "Amen" when he preaches? After all the time I have spent dedicating my life only for His kingdom and His righteousness throughout my life, it is now a great joy for me to see such time return to me as fruits.

However, sometimes when my eyes were fixed on the outcome of God's blessing, I became arrogant without even noticing it. There must not be anything to take my attention away from God, but when I fixed my eyes on the fruit of God's blessings, arrogance started to creep into my heart. Arrogance soon dominated all my thoughts.

"Oh! Our church has grown this much! I guess I'm pretty good at preaching. If this church is growing in this way, the church will soon grow into the biggest church in Busan."

Before I was aware of it, I was considering myself as the main factor for the church growth. I thought the church had grown because I preached well and dedicated myself this much. This very thought was my biggest arrogance. What is *arrogance*? It is snatching away the glory of God. Arrogance is surely a shortcut to downfall.

When I had these arrogant thoughts, it was during a Wednesday worship service time. As I stood in front of the pulpit to lead the worship service, no one showed up out of all the church members in our congregation. The church members who usually filled our sanctuary could not be seen at all as if they had promised each other not to come to church. My heart just collapsed.

"How could this happen?"

There was only my wife, the pianist and a few children in the sanctuary. Soon after I planted the church, many people came pouring into the church; still the church was merely at the starting stage. The incident, therefore, was an emergency situation. Many thoughts flashed upon me, and all kinds of anxiety piled up inside of my heart.

I did not go home that day. I could not go home. I was desperate, so I decided to pray at the pulpit until I received the answer from God. When my heart was extremely pressed, I could not do anything; rather, I did not want to do anything but pray. On the following day after leading the dawn prayer meeting, I stayed at church to pray continually and waited for the Lord's answers.

"God, I do not know what I did wrong. Please, teach me."

I waited for the Lord with the impending heart as if dying with a dry throat. How was it possible that no one came to worship all at once? I had to ask God for an answer.

"God, tell me what's going on!"

Suddenly I heard the still, small, but reprimanding voice of the Lord.

"Are you doing? I do. Are you doing? I do. Are you doing? I do."

The Lord's voice continued three times. Whenever the Lord spoke to me, it often occurred three times. Perhaps, it was because God wanted to engrave His assured and urgent will in my heart.

"Oh! My Lord! My Lord!"

I repeatedly called His name and could not do anything but repent.

"Lord, I did wrong. Lord, I did not know that You were doing everything. I thought that I was the one doing. I thought the ministry was going well because of me. Lord, it is my fault. Please, forgive me."

God spoke to me quietly.

"It was not you who established this church, but it was Me who established this church. It was not because you preached well that the church has grown, but the church was growing because I sent my people to this church."

If God sends many people, then the church becomes a big church. If He sends a small number of people, then the church becomes small. God is sovereign over the numbers.

"Lord, thank You. Thank You. Now I know. From now on, You are the Senior Pastor of this church. I will be faithful to You as an associate pastor from now on. Please take charge of this church."

From that point on, I tried to be more careful not to overstep the Lord's authority. Overstepping actions!

How often we surreptitiously try to exceed the Lord's authority! We often pretend the work entrusted by the Lord is achieved by our own efforts, and we often surreptitiously try to take the place that the Lord must take. A pastor is merely a person who has been placed in charge to take care of the Lord's sheep for a while. The pastors are the men who are doing their tasks to take care of the entrusted sheep with a thankful and grateful heart. Neither are we to overstep our boundaries nor fall short of them. In most cases, the problems rise from our irresponsibility, but sometimes the problems occur from exceeding our own authority. It is okay for pastors if they love and serve as much as the Lord wants, but the problems come when our greed is overwhelming. Overstepping our authority means intercepting the lordship in the ministry, by misunderstanding that it is the minister himself who saves and feeds the sheep.

When that happens, the Lord can no longer entrust His sheep to us. What kind of parents will entrust their child and give the rights of parents to a person who insists that your child is his? God's absolute sovereignty toward the field of pastoral ministry is the same as that. The owner of the sheep is the Lord only.

Pastors think they love their sheep, but compared with the love of the Lord, their love is just nothing. Thus, what the pastor absolutely needs is humility, and the humility must be shown through the power of love and the power of pastoral ministry. We have to love and serve not to own it for ourselves, but for the glory of God. To be faithful to the work entrusted by the Lord with a thankful and humble heart is what we must do.

"Are you doing? I do!"

After I heard the voice of the Lord, I tried not to forget always that God is the real Senior Pastor of Sooyoungro Church. Actually, I could not forget it. The one who is leading the pastoral ministry is not the pastor, but the Lord. The pastor is only a servant of the Lord.

The following Sunday after I heard the voice of the Lord, and after I repented my sins and gave back the lordship of the church, the grace of the Lord was filled evermore deeply. At that time, I understood a little how much God loves each soul, and because of that, He never gives up his sovereign authority. Parents who love their children never give up their right as parents. It was the Lord that showed His parenthood and His lordship at the most decisive moment.

However, the seats were still empty as Sunday Evening Service began. While I was leading the worship service, I prayed in my heart to the Lord.

"Lord, the back seats are empty. You need to do the home visitation right now! You're the senior pastor. Send people like driving in a swarm of quail! Who would want to come to hear my sermon? There are so many excellent pastors in good churches nearby, so who would come all the way here to hear my message? Lord, if you do not send people, no one, not even one person, will come. Since you are the one who built this church, please cover my sins and faults and please, do the home visitation now!"

Could the Lord hear my prayer? When I opened my eyes after a deacon's public prayer, people started to come pouring in the sanctuary. That particular evening, many of our church members were late to the evening worship. The seats began to fill. Looking out over the sanctuary, I said to the Lord once again.

"Lord, thank You for Your work."

Since this time, whenever I have worried about my congregation, I prayed like that. Of course, the associate pastors physically paid home visitations, but I devoted myself to a special prayer at the pulpit praying

143

like this: "Lord, I don't know why this deacon does not come to church. Lord; although I have visited his home ten times, nothing has happened. But if you visit him just once, then everything will be fine. Lord, please visit him."

When I asked the Lord with this kind of special prayer, on one occasion, a man visited my office, sharing the following testimony.

"Pastor, I'm sorry I have not come to church for a long time, but you appeared in my dream last night. I cannot stop coming to church; that is why I came to the church again."

The Lord was truly faithful. God surely visited his home and sent him back to the church as I prayed. When the Lord paid a visit to the members' houses, everything worked out well.

Since I experienced the wonderful taste of pastoral ministry, nothing was more enjoyable than pastoral ministry. Because the field of pastoral ministry was filled with God's grace, I had no reason to worry. I watched over the things that God was doing through the ministry, which made my heart overwhelmingly happy.

Expect Bigger and Greater Things for God

As the church was growing steadily by the grace of God, I continually engaged in "stepping in prayer" like the "Jericho Walk." After the dawn prayer meeting, I walked around Sooyoungro Rotary by myself and prayed to the Lord.

"Lord, give us the whole area of this rotary. Please, add this area to our church."

The area in the Rotary was like Jericho to us. We had to conquer this land with the Gospel. I believed that was the reason why God built Sooyoungro Church in the region. Whenever I prayed, I was fired up with passion to evangelize the entire city of Busan. No, it was the Holy Spirit who was praying with lament inside of me. Evangelize Busan! For that, the area of the rotary had to be evangelized first. This place had to be crumpled like Jericho. With such faith, I walked in the vicinities of the rotary every morning.

I don't recall how many years I prayed this way. As usual, that day also after the dawn prayer meeting, I walked around the rotary again in prayer and meditation of the Lord until morning. All of a sudden, I looked at the sky over Haewoondae Beach. At that moment, a bird soaring above invigoratingly in the sky caught my attention. A small bird with rather small wings kept flying high across the sky.

"It's been a long time since I saw a bird flying." At that moment, the Lord spoke to me.

"Look at the bird. Look at the space I have provided for that bird. How big and how wide is it? Doesn't the bird use the space as high as the bird flies up and as wide as the bird soars? What I have provided for you is that big and that abundant. As long as you can handle it, I will provide it as much as you need."

How could I describe my overwhelming heart at that time with words! If only I could handle it, it was the Lord who was capable of giving, not only the rotary of Sooyoungro, but even the whole world.

From that point on, I stopped walking around the rotary. The Lord gave me a promise to provide as much as I need if I could handle it. Therefore, I simply had to prepare myself, trust and wait in faith. Indeed, the promise of the Lord was accomplished soon, and I believe that the promise would continue to be accomplished from now on. The Lord actually gave the land to Sooyoungro Church, but it was more than ten times what I prayed for. The Lord also enlarged the vision of

Sooyoungro Church missions and increased the souls we had to embrace in prayers. The Lord's answer was fulfilled that much clearly.

I realized that the Lord's answer was not only clear, but also surpassed far more than our plans. We only think that everything is done when we receive things we have asked for. However, God's will and His hope are greater and mightier than our expectations.

"Open wide your mouth and I will fill it" (Psalms 81:10). God is able to do bigger and greater things willingly.

God's Work Is Done Not with Money but with One Heart

Our church has one principle when we have to handle some important matters: "If there is no opposition, God's work will be accomplished." This principle was confirmed when the church launched a new building project.

When I returned from my sabbatical year in America, the elders of the church had already bought the land behind the church. When I asked for the details, the elders told me that they bought the land as soon as it was on sale with a loan from the bank, so that others could not take advantage of the land. They arranged a payment plan with the bank to make a monthly payment and pay it off in two years. At that time, the church was riding a wave of rapid growth. After I returned from my sabbatical year, the church members increased even more, and it was impossible to hold a worship service in the current sanctuary. The elders and deacons already knew that the church could no longer accommodate all the members, so they bought the land with faithful hearts to solve the problem.

146

But the problem was money. In order to pay the loan within two years, we were not able to undertake new projects any longer. We had to build a new building on the land right away for our church members to worship. Although we checked our budget over and over, the church budget was not enough for the building project. Moreover, we could not delay the new church building project on the land because the cold winter was coming soon. If we delayed constructing the new church building, we would have to have worship in the cold weather during the winter season. We needed a temporary building at least.

Out of desperation, I cried out to the Lord for help.

"God, what shall I do? What shall I do?"

Once again, God gave me unexpended answer.

"God's work will be done if there is no objection."

Until then whenever God spoke to me, I was able to understand His answer 100 percent because He was very clear all the time. But this time, I did not understand. In order for God's work to be done, money, people, and power must accompany each other. But this time God spoke to me very strangely.

"God's work will be done if there is no objection."

God repeated these words several times, so I shared this message when we had a vestry meeting for the new church building project.

"Let us not worry if money is the issue when we have to start doing something new. You do not need to give offerings for this building project. God said everything would work out. But He said everything would work if there is no objection. I, myself, do not understand it, but since that is what God said, let us not oppose it."

All the Vestry members responded with "Amen!" We all agreed to build a 1,000 pyung (about 0.85 acre in US) sized church building without any preparation. Since all

147

the leaders agreed not to oppose it, there was no one picking arguments on this matter. Soon, we spaded the soil in the land we bought behind our old church building and started to construct the new church building. But something incredible happened. We finished the building construction within six months. How could this happen? We never made a pledge offering for the building project, and there was no prepared budget for it either. A church with 300 members spent years of preparation and finished the building project well. How could our church finish this much so soon?

When I looked at our financial report later, I found that 50 percent of the church members contributed to the offering for the building project. At that time, the attendance of our church was already several thousand, so it was made possible by half of them contributing to the building project. Then why couldn't other bigger churches in size do this? It is because there is objection. Because of objection, members are discouraged and give up before they even start.

At that time, we learned a very precious truth of God. God's work is done neither through money nor through calculation, but through one heart. God wanted to teach us this truth. If we have one heart, God evokes devoted spirits and provides for the financial needs as well.

After that experience, whenever our church built the education building or bought new land for the ministry of God, there were no objections. "If there is no objection, God's work is done" became a solid tradition of the session and of the officers of our church. No meeting was necessary. When the elders gathered together for the session meeting, they sang praises and prayed together instead of discussion, then they dismissed. Since there is no one who decided to oppose, the opinions of the pastor and the elders never conflicted. Matters were decided with unanimity and were moved on with great rapidity. Soon, those things returned to us with the abundant fruit of joy.

A Church Is Built by the Saints' Kneeling

Since then, the church expanded its land to 3,500 pyung (about 3 acres) in the Sooyoungro Rotary area. Because God's grace was so great for ten years, enlarging the church vision as well, once again we were faced with another new church building project. At that time, we agreed to build a new sanctuary of 10,000 capacity in a church parking lot that we had already bought.

However, the problem was objection. It was not from inside the church, but from the outside. It was from the surrounding neighbors. As the church was growing, traffic congestion caused a big problem every Sunday in the area of the Rotary. It was uproarious because of parking issues, and there were often locking traffic situations due to people coming to the church. The neighbors around the church harshly opposed the church construction project because they thought they would be insecure about their livelihood as the church grew.

Due to the opposition, the church reconstruction project stopped at the level of its blueprints. We, who never faced such opposition, could not help but wait for God's will.

At that time, the economic crisis called "IMF(International Monetary Fund)" took place in Korea. An urgent economic situation in this nation occurred. In this situation, something never expected happened. The eighty landowners of Woo 2 Dong located in Haewoondae-Gu (the current church location) all together came to me, asking me if Sooyoungro Church would buy their lands.

That land was the most important land around the area. Besides the wide space, it was surrounded by apartment complexes. In addition, it was located where it connected Haewoondae and Gwanganli. It served as the core of Busan. In two words, it was a golden land. The land was so big that there were eighty landowners. But why did they volunteer to sell such a great land?

The IMF at that time was the reason. Because of IMF, the real estate market was completely frozen, and those who owned land were very anxious. They thought it was best to sell the land as soon as possible to pay off the bank debt first. They were looking for the right person to sell the land to, and as a result, Sooyoungro Church was selected by them because there was a rumor that "Sooyoungro Church is a rich church."

Every day they came and urged me, "Buy the land." How could I buy the land if we did not have any savings budget? I discussed this issue in the session meeting. All the elders responded.

"We will follow your decision."

It was my turn to make a decision. At this time, I felt like God was putting a piece of cake in my mouth. If I did not eat it, I felt I would regret this forever.

The problem, then, was the budget. But actually, the money was not the problem. God had already taught me that His work would be done if there were no objections! Since I found that there was no present objection on this matter, I trusted that God would accomplish everything. With this faith, I proceeded with the work.

As expected, everything was moving along smoothly from the beginning. As we were negotiating the price of the land, we finally reached an agreement with the landowners. In fact, we bought the land at one third of the price that was originally proposed by them. It looked like the land was given to us at no cost. After we bought the land, our church members went to look at it. After they saw the land, they danced with joy. All of them in one voice shouted, "There is no land better than this." Interestingly, it was on this particular land some years ago, when we had a big Gospel rally for evangelization of Busan, all of our church members knelt on the ground for four days to pray for the goal of evangelization of fifty thousand Busan citizens. "Send us fifty thousand saints!" At that time, we prayed for our vision in tears on our knees on that reclaimed land from the sea. The Lord surely remembered that very land. And then, He gave us that land. I could not imagine how much God wanted to give the land to us! When we thought about this fact, we could not help but cry.

Soon we started with a grand scale prayer meeting. From the 24-hour relay prayer, the united prayer meeting, special prayer dawn meeting, and so on, we marched on with prayers, together with thousands of church members, making a flame of prayer. Somebody living around the church said that something like an uproar occurred every morning. At an apartment, one nonbeliever came to our church along with his neighbors (our church members) who were living in the same apartment. He was very curious because these people went to some place at four to five o'clock every morning. So he followed them because he thought something happened. In this way, he came to church and eventually became a Christian.

The background for such a grand prayer movement was from believing that we had to equip ourselves in prayer with faith for the new church building project. If we were merely caught up in the fact that we were going to build a big sanctuary, it was possible something would cause us to give up in the process. Why do churches go bankrupt, have disputes, and eventually fail in the midst of their building project? It is because the capacity of the faith of the church did not grow as much as the church grew. If big things are to be accomplished, bigger faith should be followed. If you start a big mission and do not increase your faith, you will not be able to get it done. When we pray, the same principles apply. We are often concerned mostly on how fast our prayers are answered. Compared to that, very often we do not even think about where our faith is or how much our faith is growing. But when we have enough faith, we can handle the answers from the Lord.

When the church does not prepare itself in prayer and faith, it is apt to fall into temptation before dealing with a big task. The members fall into temptation whether they decide to contribute to construction offerings or not. Disputes and divisions rise among them, and the troubles come even after they finish the building project. Therefore, before the construction of the church, the most urgent task is to equip people with faith. When equipped by faith, the saints can devote themselves to the church building project with joyful hearts. They will commit themselves and be faithful, not for someone, but for God's glory alone. It is because their eyes of faith are opened.

As we proceeded with prayer meetings in grace before starting the building project, many testimonies of prayers came out in the church. Our members, I felt, were receiving even greater gifts of joy in their lives than moving to a new church building. Getting a job, childbirth, healing, and all kinds of miraculous incidents took place in their lives.

The evidence appeared as tithes and offerings of thanksgiving. The closing balance was reported as 20 percent to 30 percent more offerings in the year of economic crisis, IMF, than in the year before. In the place of counting the annual budget, the members of the church danced with joy when they realized that God had poured out financial blessings to our church. The blessings of prayer were not limited by this. The church was filled with people praying in unity. What could not be accomplished when a church is filled with the power of praying in unity! When a place is filled with people praying with one heart, nothing can hinder them to cause a problem. There was not one who stumbled due to the building project. There was not a single problem in the entire process of actual construction. Sufficient funding for the construction was raised. The people of God and the church were firmly established.

As we prayed together with one heart, we were actually running toward the peak of the church building construction. We realized that if we were able to pray together with one heart, the evangelization of the City of Busan, unification of Korea, and evangelization of the world through this country would not be long. If we can pray together with one heart, all our dreams can become a reality.

Faith of the Saints Makes the Church Grow

In order to complete a five thousand pyung (about 4.5 acres) church, there were many people's dedication and faithfulness. The starting point of faithfulness was from an elder, the person in charge of the church building project.

He had a small business. As he became the chairman of the new church building project team, he faced many difficult situations. The neighbors were against the new construction of the church, and his business continually declined, progressively pushing toward closure. Due to his business difficulties, he kept only four employees in his company after having to let the rest go, and there seemed to be very little hope to overcome that situation. Since he was a man of prayer and a man who longed for the grace of God, he went through all the hardship as an elder. As he prayed for the church and his business, he was assured that he had to be an example of devoting himself to the Lord as the chairman of the church building committee so that the building project would continue smoothly.

One day, he came to me with an enormous check in his hands. Because I, as the pastor, knew about our church members' difficult situation, I understood very well that this offering was a big commitment and sacrifice for him since he was experiencing financial strain. Leaving his company that was on the verge of bankruptcy, he brought this check in his hands seeking God's kingdom and His righteousness first. When I saw his faith, as his pastor, tears rolled down my cheeks. I held his hands and prayed earnestly for God's blessings on him.

After some time passed, the sudden impact of the IMF became a positive factor for the elder's company, while it became a negative factor for most other companies. The value of the US dollar increased very high due to the IMF. Many businesses were seriously damaged, especially those companies that imported raw materials to make products. Because the operating funds for the company were almost exhausted and costs to buy original materials increased, most companies with tens and hundreds of employees could not function and closed down. As for the elder's company, however, he had already downsized to only four employees, so there were no more bubbles that had to be removed.

Moreover, since his competing companies closed, his company grew relatively exponentially. There were no companies to purchase such things except the elder's company. In one day, the elder's business turned around greatly like a burning fire. Later, the elder confessed the following: "It was the most successful time in my business through my life."

After that, more people continued to devote themselves to the new construction of the church with the same faith like the elder. The faith of Sooyoungro Church members grew in that way.

There was a woman of faith who came with a big offering during the evening even though her husband was sick in bed. There were men and women of faith who were too embarrassed to make their offerings with names because they thought it was a very small amount. Whether rich or poor, everybody gave their offerings with such hearts to break their precious jar of perfume in order to give it to the Lord. With that heart, they gave their money and time. It was the faith of Sooyoungro Church.

Faith is not looking at the problem, but looking at the Lord. Even when difficult issues that we cannot handle well come into our lives, if the faith looking at the Lord grows bigger, the problem becomes smaller. Faith grows bigger, God grows bigger inside of us, and the problem loses its place in our life. One day the problem disappears. People of faith should deal with problems in that way. If we resolve the problem in faith, the problem must be resolved.

Before the construction of the church building began, we acquired that kind of faith through the grand prayer meetings. And with that faith, people voluntarily made their devotion to the Lord. If we simply looked at hardships and difficult situations, then no one was able to devote himself to the Lord, but when looking at the Lord, we could do it with joyful hearts. From there, we were able to experience God's abundant blessings.

Before the construction of the new church building, I never mentioned anything to the congregation about making pledge offerings for the construction. I preached only the words of faith. I never told them about my concerns for the church. I only asked them not to worry about anything, but only to devote themselves to prayer. When the pastor worries, everyone in the congregation will worry. Worry is contagious so that as a result people do not do God's work with joyful hearts. However, if the pastor looks to the Lord with faith, then the congregation looks at the work of the Lord with faith. If the pastor initiates God's work with calculation, then the congregation will do the work of the Lord with calculation. Therefore, because it is the work of the Lord, we have to do the work with faith and with a pure heart.

At that time, we did not even allow anyone to make a pledge for the building offering. I taught the church members not to contribute offerings if they did not have a joyful and voluntary heart because a pledge by force would be very foolish. It was my true heart. I did not want to restrain church members using the church construction project. Even if it is God's work, if people make devotions by force from the pastor without a voluntary heart, then it will return to the pastor and to the congregation as a restraint. It becomes a big burden. Because I knew this, I only asked people to pray to receive grace and for a progress of faith.

People voluntarily devoted themselves to the Lord, and the construction of the church building progressed very smoothly and excitingly. The offering was overflowing, and the construction went very well without any accidents or mistakes.

But that was not all. It was confirmed over and over during the construction that the building site was the best land of all as God's provision. Because the site was a landfill that covered the sea, we dug the stale roof very deep. Everywhere that we dug, there was rock. It was rock originally in the sea. The church built on the rock! It indicated just our church. We wondered about water leaking because it was a landfill, but there was no water to leak. All the water from the land went down to the subway construction that had taken place previously. The soil was hard, and inside the land was firm. There, we built the sanctuary building with a 1.5 meter waterproof wall, driven with iron pillars that connected the structure like an ark. Because it was just after the IMF crisis, the construction company gave their best in construction, bringing all the equipment they had because they did not have businesses due to IMF.

After two years of construction, we dedicated to God the beautifully finished new church building. Without anyone falling into temptation because of the construction, the church was completed, being filled and overwhelmed without anything lacking. It was evidence that the faith of the saints in our congregation grew that much.

Through this experience, Sooyoungro Church was able to have even greater faith that allowed for even greater things. It was an opportunity for the members to examine how great their faith was in God. In this way, the construction of the new church building made Sooyoungro Church's vision grow even greater.

CHAPTER 7

Maturity: Grace Increases As Much As We Share

Enlarge Your Prayer Bosom

After construction of the new church building, the area that Sooyoungro Church needed to focus on was maturity. Often times, when a church reaches a certain level of growth, they even forget the reason why the church needs to grow, and they move forward merely "to reach a goal with a certain number." At that point, if a church does not take another step towards maturity, it tends to lose the pure calling of the church. Forgetting the reason why the church was built, there is a tendency to fall into selfishness of individualism of the church. Therefore, as the church progresses into a stage of growth, a paradigm of maturity must be brought appropriately. Passion for the revival inside of the church must be changed to the outside of the church in order to share the blessings that have been received so far. When such a matured serving is continued, the church can experience a balanced revival.

With this principle, we prepared to build a center at the Sooyoung rotary with longing for holiness for the whole city of Busan, and with the burning desire to serve local communities as well as this country. For this, we tried to systemize all of our programs and direction of ministry for serving churches throughout Korea, and at the same time, we gathered prayers and interest of the whole congregation. We defined maturity as a serving and giving church for everyone who visits our church from across the world, so that they can be satisfied both physically and spiritually and return to their places.

For mature service, it is important to have that kind of church system. However, it is more important to serve with words and prayers that are faithful from the inside. Behind the growth of Sooyoungro Church, I have often sensed the prayers of church members who have prayed for me by fasting and shedding tears. In the Korean Church, there must be such a service of prayer. As a church that has been given a special task of praying, I hope that all the members of our church will kindle the fire of prayer, embracing the churches in Korea in their hearts. I am sure that this wish is gradually being fulfilled. When we are praying together with one heart, there is nothing to stop the ministry of the Lord. We have already experienced this when we were constructing the new church building. Once the prayers are gathered, materials, workforces, and devotions are provided sufficiently. Now, our church hopes to be the vessel of prayer so that we can send such a message to the churches in Korea.

A missionary's story verifies this process very well. The missionary was serving at a small hospital at that time. One day, he received a donation to use for the hospital and was on the way back to his ministerial field with a Chinese helper. As they were heading back, they needed to stay at a camp that night in the mountain because it was already dark. They felt uneasy because the area was infamous for bandits, but they put their trust in the Lord and prayed for God's protection for the money that belonged to God. The next morning, they thanked God for keeping themselves and the money safe, and returned safely to the hospital. Shortly after that incident, the head of the bandits came to the hospital. While he was receiving the treatment, the man saw the missionary and asked, "Did you go to a city to bring some money a few weeks ago?"

"Yes, I did. How did you know that?"

"At that time, you camped outside with guards in the mountain, right?"

"Wait a minute! Did you say guards?"

"We were planning to rob you, but we could not because twenty-seven guards were surrounding you."

"What? Only my colleague and I stayed there."

It was very strange. The missionary and the Chinese helper's statements must be true. But the man said, "Guards!" This man's statements seemed to be true as well because he mentioned a specific number of guards.

Later, when the missionary spoke at a Gospel rally in England, the mystery became fully clear. At the rally, one man who attended spoke.

"That night, we gathered at the church and prayed for you. The people who were gathered at the prayer meeting were twenty-seven people."

I sincerely trust and hope that this kind of testimony pours out from the saints in our congregation. When the saints are praying, I dreamt that trumpet sounds of the Gospel are echoed through the whole city of Busan, idols are being destroyed throughout Korea, and missionaries are bringing the messages of victories from all around the world. Because of that, the saints of

Sooyoungro Church should not stop serving in prayers because serving in prayers is our calling.

Stop Counting and Remember That One Soul Is More Precious than the Whole World

If the congregation of Sooyoungro Church serves by prayer for the whole world, then as a pastor, with what should I serve? Thinking of the task, I began to confess. "Lord, I know I am a deficient servant, but I will go and run all around the world with your words."

It was a confession that I would completely give myself as an instrument of the Holy Spirit and go to any church or any place wherever people needed me. This is the main reason why I refrain from meals and do not even turn on the TV whenever I lead special revival rallies outside of my church. At this time, no matter what kind of special rallies, I just focus on prayers unifying my heart, will, and sincerity.

"Lord, please pour out the great grace upon this revival rally!"

From the first revival rally I led until now, I never miss this prayer. How fearful and gratifying it is to be used by God to revive one soul or thousands of souls that God has entrusted to me with the Word of God! Probably, most preachers who are leading the revival rallies will have the same heart.

However, while I am leading the revival rallies in different places, sometimes I get heartbroken because from time to time, I meet some pastors who have already fallen into materialism.

On one occasion, I was leading a revival rally at a foreign country. It was a united revival rally that several churches were working together. The revival rally was held in quite a large sanctuary; however, when I stood on the pulpit, I found that not many people showed up for the rally. Since it was a united revival rally at a big sanctuary, many empty seats made the church look even bigger, and the host members looked deeply embarrassed. However, if the glory of God fills this place, why should the attendance numbers be a problem? Even if there is only one person, it is the Lord surely to receive the glory through him! Since I did not have any worries about the number in attendance, I did my best to preach the Word of God. In fact, those who were gathered in that sanctuary sought God's grace more sincerely, and I was able to deliver the Word of God joyfully and happily.

When the first night of revival rally was over, everyone's face was shining. Then the hosting pastor told me about an incident at the united revival rally one year ago. They invited a very well-known pastor to lead the united revival rally at that church; however, just like tonight, not many people showed up. The guest pastor became angry.

"Do you know how busy I am? Since you all invited me, what are you doing without any preparation?"

Through his rebuke, all the people in the rally just wanted to hide, even in a mouse hole. When the rally started that evening, they said they were so nervous because they saw that the attendance was fairly low again just as the previous year. But everyone said that they were moved greatly by my attitude to deliver the word of God very joyfully. Then after the service, they voluntarily called every member's homes. The very next day, unbelievably, the sanctuary was filled with many people, and we experienced the grace of the rally together.

At that time, I thought again about how many pastors have fallen into materialism. When I am traveling to lead revival rallies in a country like Japan, often I can see pastors who come to church at three in the morning to pray for three hours. Although pastors like them are doing their ministry with tears every day, the actual attendance at the rally is low. It is because there are very few people who were chosen by the Lord around them. In that situation, there are many servants who take a step forward day by day with silence for the Kingdom of the Lord and His righteousness. Therefore, if a pastor becomes angry watching over and counting people, he is not a servant anymore, but rather acts as the lord.

Often, we also have such attitudes when we are doing the pastoral ministry. First of all, we begin the ministry to serve, but as time goes by, we often become a pastor who does his ministry to boast. Therefore, we have to check ourselves whether we have not been changed as such a pastor or not.

Those who truly serve well are those who have a simple heart.

"Lord, thank you for the opportunity you have given me to preach the words before the souls that are more precious than the whole world."

"Lord, thank you for the blessing that I have something to share."

People who have such a heart can share anytime.

A large tree provides the grace of luxuriant leaves to take a rest for one person or ten people unsparingly. And when the fall season comes, it produces the most healthy and abundant fruits. As much as we share with pure and genuine hearts, the fruits will be true and genuine.

What kind of pastor am I? Am I a mature servant to do my best faithfully toward anything entrusted to me? Or, am I the opposite? As I travel around to serve for the Korean churches or churches around the world, many incidents I experienced eventually challenge me to reflect upon myself.

The Grace of God Grows the More We Share

Once we had a retreat gathering missionaries in our denomination for three nights and four days. God taught me some precious truth during that particular retreat. At the place I went to serve, I received the biggest gift and returned.

Since I understood how difficult the missionary fields were, I focused my sermons on unity and love among co-workers. After the programs, I asked them to hug each other. An atmosphere of forgiveness and love began to fill the place as time passed—one hour, two hours, one day, and two days. At the end, they looked at each other in love with tears. The grace given by the Holy Spirit was tremendous throughout the retreat.

However, there was one missionary that would not open up his heart from the beginning to the end. As the preacher, I had been worrying about this missionary continually.

I prayed: "Lord, what shall I do? One person's soul is deeply wounded."

I could not get him out of my thoughts during the sermons and even after all the programs were over. I had no idea why only this missionary was having problems when everyone around him was moved in overflowing grace of the Lord. Moreover, I wondered how he could work as a missionary in that situation. I expected his hard and burdened heart to be melted through the retreat.

Finally, I called him and tried to express my heart to him, giving some encouraging support. I had hoped to recover his heart at the very least. However, he was not moved at all.

Then, I had ill intuitions that suddenly sprang into my mind. I felt that if I left him in this state, something bad might happen to him. It was a very strange sense of foreboding.

So during the break time, my wife and I went back to our room at the retreat center, and we knelt down. My wife, on her bed, and I, on my bed, had a special prayer meeting for the missionary. With loving hearts, we prayed for him embracing his soul.

"Lord, I think he should not leave in this situation. Please heal his wounded heart and the scars inside of him. Lord, please revive him!"

When the hurt and pains in a minister's heart are not melted, then the trace of his deep hurt and pain must be from his ministerial field. I prayed to God for him so that his heart would be filled with love and a forgiving heart.

At that moment, instantaneously, a realization came into my mind like lightning. A truth that I never thought or realized before dug into my heart. It was about the arrogance that had been rooted deeply inside of me. What kind of person am I? I was the most arrogant one among the arrogant ones. Serving as the class leader when I was young, I often judged my friends with my own standards.

After a test, when I was grading the papers by the teacher's request, I often judged students.

"This guy better to go to this school . . . this guy's score is 80!"

"This guy is so stupid. How can he only get this grade?"

Those moments were all sinful moments because I judged the level of human beings just with grades.

"That guy is a good man."

"That guy is a right person."

"That guy should perished."
"That guy must not be well."
Oh, I have lived judging people in that way. Somehow, without realizing it, I was trying to be God. Sometimes even if I did not have a quarrel or dispute with someone, but if there were some points that were not fit for my standards, I put hateful feelings in a corner of my heart. If I have that kind of mind, people can read my heart, no matter how hard I try to hide it. The truth must be apparent somewhere on my face or in my way of speaking. Looking back, I thought that I had lived creating my enemies by myself. Although I have grown receiving much love from many people, this was the reason that there were always one or two enemies. My standards to judge made by myself appeared in my face, and I received dislike and misunderstanding from people. I thought, "Why does that person hate me without a reason?" But because I had committed sin by judging them first, that was the reason why they hated me.

"Do not judge, or you too will be judged! For in the same way you judge others, you will be judged, and with the same measure you use, it will be measured to you" (Matthew 7:1–2).

This verse tells us not to judge or not to evaluate others like a judge. A person we view as an "ugly duckling" in our eyes can become a beautiful swan that God uses. It is only God who can judge people, but we do not know how often we commit sin trying to be God in our lives.

In a short time, the Holy Spirit helped me to see the roots of my arrogance. When I was praying with love for the missionary who judged and condemned me, the Holy Spirit instead guided me to realize my own faults. So to speak, through the missionary, the

Holy Spirit helped me to see my sinful nature from my childhood, and He taught me not to judge those who were on trial by me or those who hate me. On the contrary, the Holy Spirit taught me the fact that if I lift them up only with prayers of blessings and love, everything will end beautifully.

When I realized this fact within such a short time, I was so overwhelmed with joy. I felt just as if I were flying. I shared this testimony with my wife who was praying beside me. "Honey, the Holy Spirit helped me to realize a truth worth ten thousand dollars!" and my wife replied, "It is more than one hundred thousand dollars!"

That moment, I met God, the Holy Spirit, who looks even inside of our hearts. I met the faithful God who wants the sincerity of the heart. I met the God who wants us to take care of His sheep, not with a disguised kindness or disguised expressions, but with a sincere blessing and loving heart. When you are taking care of the flock of sheep, if you do not judge them, and if you always bless them with love, those who have been hostile to you will be changed in the end, and eventually they will come back to you. That was what God taught me.

God allowed such a bonus to me in that way. He solved the problems that might be a thorn or suffering through my pastoral life in a moment. A pastor is not a man of judging, but must be a man of blessing and a man of loving always. Helping me realize this fact, God was leading our pastoral, ministerial field as a field of love. After this incident, whenever I met people who were in serious trials or troubles, I was able to be a pastor who prayed to God kneeling down completely, blessing them.

"Father, I don't know why the deacon is so upset, but I think he is definitely in a trial. I don't know what I did wrong, Lord, but I love that person so much. Please go and meet with him and let him know my heart. Please allow him a heart to forgive me."

I prayed for him like that until the sign of enmity or grievance toward me disappeared in his face. Surprisingly, then the problem was solved, and often they visited with this confession.

"Pastor, I was in trial because of you. But during the worship today, the Holy Spirit talked to me in my heart to go and ask you for forgiveness."

As the number of church members increases, unexpected incidents occur, and some members fall into trials by them. Some get upset by saying that I ignored greeting them, or some fall into trial arguing that their name was missing on an announcement. When a member is in trial by a pastor, it is the member himself who suffers the most. Because they have no joy in church life, they do not receive grace even though they have the words. To be blessed with a life in faith, they must solve this problem as soon as possible.

Pastors should not provide any reason for church member to fall into trials. And yet, if there is a man who still goes around slandering the pastor, the pastor must pray for him, embracing him with blessing unconditionally because no one should be allowed to stumble.

The Lord truly has taught me a very precious truth of pastoral ministry through the incident of the retreat. When I prayed for the missionary who hated me, embracing him with love, the Lord gave me such a bonus.

After a while, when I met the missionary again, his face had been changed to a face of an angel! He told us that he had gone through a serious car accident that almost killed him. As we prayed, the field of his heart was changed into a soft soil. At that time, we did not know, but my wife and I prayed for him. "Please save the missionary from the coming trial." "Please change his heart so that he can do his work well." God has touched me in that way. In that sense, the retreat still remains in my heart as an unforgettable time. Maybe it proves the Korean saying, "If it is shared, it will get bigger." When I share one blessing to ten people, then the one blessing will become ten different meanings. Not only that, when you kneel down before God with a heart to share one thing, then the Lord will show one hundred things. Like this, as much as you share, the man who shares is raised as a bigger servant before the Lord.

If a church is mature, she wants to share many more things in the future. I will continue to bless the churches in Korea and serve through prayers, and the Lord will use such churches even more greatly. I sincerely pray for Sooyoungro Church to be such a church, and that I will first become such a pastor.

CHAPTER 8

Power: The Ability Of A Pastoral Ministry Is Piety

Seeds of Piety Are in Godly Words

Sooyoungro Church is located in Busan, but many saints all around Korea often visit our church. In order to attend many different seminars and rallies for pastors and laity every Monday, there are always many people that are not only from Busan, but also from all around Korea. When I look at their zeal for the Kingdom of God and His righteousness, I have been deeply challenged and blessed. However, they often ask me these questions.

"What's the key to Sooyoungro Church's blessings?"

"The Holy Spirit has done everything. There really isn't a secret."

"Then how do we work for the ministry with the Holy Spirit?"

"You must become an instrument of the Holy Spirit."

"What should we do to be an instrument of the Holy Spirit?"

I probably do not even need to answer the question. If anyone meditates on who the Holy Spirit is, he can easily have the answer to that. Who is the Holy Spirit? He is the *Holy* Spirit. Therefore, if one wants to do the ministry with the Holy Spirit, then he must keep only one thing: holiness, namely, a holy life!

When pastors ask me what we need the most in the pastoral ministry, without hesitation, I answer that it is "piety." It is not capability or talents. It is piety. Piety is truly the life for pastors.

The reason that pastors often feel that ministry is hard or fail in the ministry is because they do not keep a godly lifestyle. It is a great paradox if a pastor expects the Holy Spirit to use him although he is living an ungodly life. Living a holy life should be a priority, and we can then live as instruments of the Holy Spirit.

"Don't you know that you yourselves are God's temple and that God's Spirit dwells in your midst? If anyone destroys God's temple, God will destroy that person; for God's temple is sacred, and you together are that temple" (1 Corinthians 3:16–17).

As the verse says, our body is the temple of God. Therefore, if holiness is broken, the Holy Spirit mourns because He cannot use us.

The evidence of a godly life usually comes from our words. From a person's words in normal conversations, not in careful conversations with great attention paid intentionally, can be understood clearly his current situation of piety. Is he speaking words of peace, thankfulness, encouragement, blessings, and humbleness?

Or is he speaking words of people's faults, pride, worry, lewdness, and complaint?

When you are living a godly life, there is no way to boast about yourself. You do not lift yourself up as if you are a hero, but you always lift God up highly.

"Humble yourselves, therefore, under God's mighty hand, that he may lift you up in due time" (1 Peter 5:6). We are considered worthy and precious because of God. However, we are not the ones to be praised. Therefore, we must always remember that Jesus is the only one who is worthy to be praised.

If a person always uses words of fear and criticism, then it is proof that he is not living a godly life. Christians are the people who have the authority over words. , The pastor's words especially determine the ambience of the church. If the pastor delivers words of hopelessness, then the church falls into a hopeless ambience. However, in the midst of hardship, when a pastor speaks with hopeful words, then the church becomes filled with hope. The Holy Spirit is the Spirit of hope. One who lives with the Holy Spirit will not lose peace and joy in the midst of hardship. He is joyful and happy. We should not forget that is the power of piety.

"Rejoice in the Lord always. I will say it again: Rejoice!" (Philippians 4:4).

In that case, if a person uses words as a weapon to attack, that is evidence of a lack of holiness. It has been said that those who use a sword will be destroyed by the sword.

The pastor who tries to control the congregation by words and church members who try to control the pastor by words lead to destruction of the church. When a problem arises, if a man tries to solve the problem only with words, often he tumbles down by the trap of the words. Is there anyone who presents a note and says, "You surely said this in that month and on that day!" If a pastor did that, he loses the virtue as a pastor at the time he said that. Who would come to the pastor? Who opens his heart before the pastor? Pastors should forgive and cover any problems according to the Word of God. Then, the Holy Spirit will solve the problem and lead the field of pastoral ministry to prevent any trouble that might occur in the future.

Those who enjoy obscene words or those who are not able to give up obscene habits are people who lack piety. The ministerial fields of such pastors are mostly not graceful. They are apt to be caught in turmoil during their ministry even if things are going well for a while. Sometimes they are misunderstood, as though they have violated the seventh commandment.

The Holy Spirit desires the servants of God to have godly lips. He seeks for servants who are eager to share God's grace whenever they open their mouths. Of course, because pastors are human beings, they make mistakes too. However, if we live within the grace of God, we are such people who are able to say godly things in our daily living. Those who are in love want to speak with those whom they love even for twenty-four hours. We are the people who fall in love with the Lord. Then, our lives must be filled with His stories. We must not fill our lives enjoying conversations about our enemies that cause us to stumble.

In that aspect, pastors should avoid obscene jokes or words of impatience because it brings many mistakes. In my opinion, it is the best attitude that pastors should listen more, praise or encourage people in their communications, and smile occasionally.

"Let your conversation be always full of grace, seasoned with salt, so that you may know how to answer to everyone" (Colossians 4:6).

However, God uses every temperament and character. It does not matter whether we are introverted or extroverted as long as we are clothed with "holiness." There is no best character or temperament for the pastor separately. Eventually, a pastor is determined as good or not by being clothed with holiness in his temperament.

For this, pastors should develop a good habit of godly speech. The reason I encourage church members to share graceful conversations with others as much as possible is that it will eventually bear more graceful conversations. In the same way, if pastors or church members share obscene jokes, the jokes grow bigger and the spirit of obscenity starts to work within them. Eventually, their holy lips become a tool of obscenity.

This applies not just to pastors, but also to pastors' wives, elders, and deacons equally. Most people in the world think that they are innocent as long as they do not have any sins appearing outwardly. They criticize the younger generation who go to bars, but they do not take it seriously when the mature members of the church have obscene conversations in the church unreservedly. Working already as servants of Satan, they are busy judging everyone else.

The reason for all of this is because of the lack of respect and fear of the Lord. Those who fear the Lord do not just abhor evil things but run away from the evil itself. By doing so, they dedicate themselves to the Lord as instruments of the Holy Spirit.

> "In a large house there are articles not only of gold and silver, but also of wood and clay; some are for noble purposes and some for ignoble. If a man cleanses himself from the latter, he will be instruments

for noble purposes, made holy, useful to
the Master and prepared to do any good
work" (2 Timothy 2:20–21).

This verse shows what kind of people God uses as
precious instruments. According to these words, the
only and the most important things for a servant of God
are "to be holy" and "to be cleansed."
That is all that we have to do. Wisdom, power, grace,
and gifts—all these things are to be given by the Holy
Spirit. All we can do is to keep ourselves clean so that
the Holy Spirit comes to us with joy and uses us fully.
The apostle Paul told Timothy to train himself to
be godly.

"Have nothing to do with godless myths
and old wives' tales; rather, train yourself to be godly. For physical training is
of some value, but godliness has value
for all things, holding promise for both
the present life and the life to come" (1
Timothy 4:7–8).

Why did he say to train himself in this way? It is
because we have a tendency to lose godliness if we do
not endeavor to train ourselves with all our heart. It is
the same concept as getting dirty after a long day even
though we take a shower every day. Only one hour at
a dusty place will make our whole body dirty. Likewise,
our godliness can be lost instantly. Satan waits for this
kind of opportunity and then rushes to us like a roaring
lion, trying to swallow us. When piety is lost, we become
Satan's servant in defenseless situations.

Godliness Is the Power and Real Ability

When I lived in the United States of America for two years during the sabbatical years, I realized how much the power of godliness of a pastor was important. In 1982, seven years after I started pastoral ministry, I was allowed a sabbatical year from the church and went to study in America with my family. During this time, upon rising I prayed for an hour every morning, and I did not neglect meditating on God's Word. However, was it possible that I was spending too much time studying? Or was it because my life pattern had changed from shepherding the flock of the sheep and meditating on the Lord for twenty-four hours a day? I began to feel dryness in my heart, and I could not control it. Later, I felt my heart was like a barren desert. I did not understand the reason why I felt that kind of spiritual thirst when I was eating, sleeping, and resting well. My heart that had once been filled fully with the Holy Spirit seemed to be totally empty.

One day, I decided to check my own spiritual state. A sense of crisis came into my mind that I could not continue my ministry any longer if this situation lasted any longer. If I lived with this kind of spiritual dryness during my sabbatical year, I might earn a doctorate degree, but I felt my ministry would not be blessed. I was about to die due to a total spiritual dehydration, but how was it that I could do the pastoral ministry in this situation?

Who is a pastor? A pastor is a person who should not live without God's grace even for a moment. There is no hope for his ministerial field without grace. Only when the ministry is flooded with the waters of grace are the thirsty sheep able to come and drink to renew their strength. That is the revival. Therefore, if you desire revival in the church, grace must be present first. It is the reason why a pastor's priority should be to always live by the river of grace.

Remembering this, I reset my priority before God once again. Although the studies were important, praying enough so that my soul would not dry out before God was more important. One hour of prayer and one hour of Scripture reading a day was not enough. I decided to study after I had enough time to pray and to read the Word of God. This is the same for our ministries. If we do our ministry without taking enough time for the scripture and prayer, before we see the revival of our ministerial fields, the body and soul of the pastor will perish first.

Early the next morning, since I could not find any churches around the area to attend for dawn prayer services, I went outside and crawled into a small playhouse that looked like a doghouse. It was a small space where children could play inside. When I went in with my head down, I could not stand up because my head reached the top, but it was a very good place for me to pray. Ever since I found this perfect place, I set the playhouse as my prayer room. Every day at the break of dawn, I prayed sometimes one hour, sometimes two hours, sometimes three hours until my heart was saturated with the Lord.

Recovery came to me in that way. When I started to pray, it was still dark outside at dawn. But when I came out from the playhouse, the sun was shining brightly. The morning dew glittered from the sunshine, and my soul glittered from the tears of my prayers. When I read the scriptures with such a glittering heart, I am filled with God's grace.

Afterward I began to study. By the way, some great thing happened. Since I was restored in grace before God, my study in English improved. In the same way as my studies had improved after I received Jesus in elementary school, I could see a noticeable progress in my studies after my tired soul was recovered by grace, even if I studied for a short time. To write a term paper is not easy, even if writing in our mother tongue. However, with a clearer head and better concentration, I was able to write the difficult term paper in English quite well. From that time, even room in my heart appeared. I did not have room in my mind because I was too busy praying and reading the Word, but once I took time enough to focus on the prayer and Word, plenty of room appeared in my heart.

I don't know how the churches in the United States knew about my staying in the country. From that time, many different churches asked me to lead revival rallies every single week. I was invited by churches in Chicago, Greensboro, Cleveland, and many other churches from different cities that I had never known before. I really did not have any idea how the churches even from different denominations got my telephone number. Sometimes, I led the revival rallies twice a week. The requests to lead revival rallies continued until I went back to Korea. As I began to live in God's grace during the sabbatical years, God helped me share the grace of God to others in that way.

At that time, I learned a lesson once again. If any servants of God are ready in preparation, God uses them preferentially. If a servant is soaked in God's grace in their souls, God does not let him sit idle. Because it is urgent to share the Gospel, and there are many places to be blessed, there are very few servants who are filled by the grace in their souls, and that is why God is eager to find His servants.

Piety, therefore, is a lifeline for pastors. If piety is practiced, God will use His servant abundantly. Since

178

piety is so important, Satan attacks pastors from all sides to destroy their piety, so pastors need to pull an oar more to the sea of grace, seeking more grace from God.

A person who experiences God's grace even once will experience feelings of depression if they do not live continually in the deep grace of God. It is the same reason why a person who enjoys swimming in the deep sea no longer enjoys swimming in the shallow waters. Pastors are such people. They must go continually into the deep waters of grace and be soaked in the sea of grace, so that they will not dry out and can continue to deliver grace to the sheep. The goal, therefore, of the pastor is not to increase the number of members. The goal must be to go to the deeper ocean of grace in order to have deeper fellowship with the Lord. God is looking for such a pastor who has such a goal even today.

> The mercy of God is an ocean divine, a boundless and fathomless flood;
> Launch out in the deep, cut away the shoreline,
> And be lost in the fullness of God.
> Launch out into the deep, O, let the shoreline go,
> Launch out, launch out in the ocean divine, Out where the full tides flow.
> But many, alas! Only stand on the shore, And gaze on the ocean so wide;
> They never have ventured its depths to explore,
> Or to launch on the fathomless tide.
> Launch out into the deep, O, let the shoreline go,
> Launch out, launch out in the ocean divine, Out where the full tides flow.
> And others just venture away from the land, And linger so near to the shore,

179

That the surf and the slime that beat over the strand, Dash o'er them in floods evermore.
Launch out into the deep, O, let the shoreline go, Launch out, launch out in the ocean divine, Out where the full tides flow.
O, let us launch out on this ocean so broad, Where floods of salvation o'er flow;
O, let us be lost in the mercy of God, Till the depths of His fullness we know.
Launch out into the deep, O, let the shoreline go, Launch out, launch out in the ocean divine, Out where the full tides flow. (Korean Hymn 408)

Two Wings of Piety: The Words and Prayer

Samson was a man with a large and robust frame and more handsome than any other. Who could have surpassed Samson's strength and his physical attractiveness? But he made a decisive mistake. He slept laying his head on the lap of Delilah.

He failed not because his hair had been cut. When he laid his head down on the lap of a prostitute, it was almost the same as his life ending. As a Nazirite, who must have a holy life, Samson threw his holiness away by himself.

Similarly, if pastors lose their godliness, they will lose everything. The Holy Spirit will not be able to work, and at the same time, the respect from the saints will vanish. That is the life of pastors. Pastors cannot receive the respect and love of others by demanding, "Serve me! Respect me!" Rather, pastors will be respected and loved when church members recognize their lives are acceptable from their hearts.

Then, how can we become such pastors?

It is through piety. The power to shine as a pastor is piety. The strength and power of piety produce the real power for the ministry. If a pastor lives in that way, even if he meets tribulation and collapses time to time, eventually he will receive the crown of victory. At first, the power of piety might be seemingly weak, but it will work as the greatest power in the end because the power of piety comes from the help of the Holy Spirit. Such men of piety are "genuine, yet regarded as impostors; known, yet regarded as unknown; dying, and yet they live on; beaten, and yet not killed; sorrowful, yet always rejoicing; poor, yet making many rich; having nothing, and yet possessing everything" (2 Corinthians 6:8–10). Such a pastor will surely receive respect and love from many people.

On the contrary, those who live a life following the desires of their bodies are "genuine, yet regarded as impostors; known, yet regarded as unknown; living, and yet they are dead; rejoicing, yet always sorrowful; making many rich, yet always poor; possessing everything, and yet having nothing." The fields of pastoral ministry are the places where the Holy Spirit works. Therefore, pastors cannot deceive church members.

The only attractive asset that pastors should pursue is piety. This attraction cannot be shown artificially. No one can pretend to be holy. But once you live godly, no matter how hard you try to cover yourself with humbleness, the attraction and the power of piety must appear. Just as the dead body gives off rotten smells even if wrapped well, a living man cannot conceal himself even if he is pretending to be dead. A man of piety gives off the fragrance of Jesus Christ even if he does not have talent, degree, and wealth. People will say when they see such a pastor, "Our pastor is truly a man who is filled by grace. He lives in grace."

181

The evaluation of a pastor's life is not decided by showmanship or pretense. The true evaluation is naturally formulated through being together for a long period of time. In that sense, in a husband-wife relationship, if a spouse says, "My husband (or wife) is truly a man (or a woman) who is living fully in the grace of God," that man (or wife) is truly a man (or a woman) of power. The man whose life is full of grace, who cannot love such a man?

That is why the Apostle Paul struggled to obey, disciplining himself for the godly life. It is difficult for even married people to keep their piety, so it must have been harder for the Apostle Paul, living as a single man his entire life. However, he lived a holy life to the end, disciplining himself and obeying, so that he would not be abandoned by God. That is the difference between Paul and others.

The servant of God must be like this. He should make every effort to keep piety in spite of the fact that he is weak in many areas. Even if he is a little homely, even if he is not able to preach well, if he tries to keep piety in his life, the amazing work of the Lord will appear. The power of the Holy Spirit appears through the pastor's inarticulate sermon, and people come into the small sanctuary. The work of revival that cannot be understood by the human mind appears.

Because this precious thing is the power of piety, greater faith, wisdom, and determination are required to maintain this piety. In other words, a holy life can never be achieved without spiritual battles. For that, pastors should spend hours in God's Word and in prayer always. Often a pastor emphasizes a life with prayer and the Word of God. However, it is very hard for the pastor himself to keep the life with the Word of God and prayer regularly. It is not easy to reach the level where a pastor prays like he is breathing, and he reads the Word like he is breathing because there is the tyranny of many urgent things in the pastoral ministry. If a pastor is not built up in God's Word and prayer, he is not able to do pastoral ministry powerfully. Therefore, these two things must unfold to receive power for the ministry. The Bible describes this clearly.

"They forbid people to marry and order them to abstain from certain foods, which God created to be received with thanksgiving by those who believe and who know the truth. For everything God created is good, and nothing is to be rejected if it is received with thanksgiving because it is consecrated by the word of God and prayer" (1 Timothy 4:3–5).

To have holiness, it is not important whether we eat something or not, or whether we get married or not. Rather, it is crucial to receive power in the Word and prayer. Rather than to do something or not, it is more necessary to meet the Lord fully in His Word and in prayer.

Several years ago, I realized this important lesson while fasting. At that time, I was very busy at the church, so I was not able to pray while I fasted. Simply, it was a time when I just skipped meals. It was hard for me because I was fasting while fulfilling many duties at the same time. I was just starving. As the days passed, I did not even feel that hungry anymore. So, I even thought, "Oh, maybe this is how they do the forty day fasting prayer." By that time, I never fasted for a long time because while I was praying for three to four days, God always answered my prayer soon. However, that time, the length of fasting was long, but I actually did not have enough time to pray. I had to finish my fasting without gaining any kind of meaning. Simply fasting itself, marriage itself, or working busily in your ministry field itself cannot give us power. It only provides more opportunities to be tempted by sin. Therefore, the goal in our daily lives is a daily routine of God's Word and prayer. To live while praying becomes like breathing and meditating on the Word of God becomes food, which must be the first goal of our life. When it is, our spirit will be filled like a wide ocean.

When the pastor's spirit is filled fully by grace, the pulpit where the preaching is delivered and the church where the pastoral ministry is operated become the field of grace. Transformation in a pastor brings change in the whole church.

One Good Thought Can Change Life

When a pastor focuses on God's Word and prayer for a godly life, the first thing he must overcome is the area of *thinking*. Thinking is the most sensitive and clear place that our spiritual condition can be measured because it is the birthplace for our words and actions. Thoughts enter our mind without any boundaries. It would be great if only good thoughts or graceful thoughts came in, but it is a reality that bad thinking, dirty thinking, and useless thinking come as well. If we consider it carefully, there is no bigger war than such a war. Inner mind or inside thoughts rush into fierce battle constantly.

Some say that "thinking is free," but thoughts should not be left alone because they form our habits, and habits decide our lives. Therefore, we should be following the thoughts of the Holy Spirit as much as we can. When we do that, we can bear the fruits of the Holy Spirit. "So I say, walk by the Spirit, and you will not gratify the desires of the sinful nature" (Galatians 5:16). We have thoughts from the Holy Spirit and thoughts from the devil. The thoughts that come suddenly to our mind are unavoidable. However, if greed settles in our mind, there is a tendency to repeat thoughts of the flesh and eventually make us commit a sin against the Holy Spirit. On the contrary, if we think repeatedly according to the desire of the Holy Spirit, we can bear the fruits of the Holy Spirit. This means that we can choose a repeated meditation without limit. Thoughts are the object that can be conquered and have to be conquered.

Among people, there are many who succeed in life because of one good thought, and there are some who fail because of just one single bad thought. What kind of mind you have or what you think in a critical moment determines the whole life. The Bible proves this fact: "Like a city whose walls are broken down is a man who lacks self-control" (Proverbs 25:28).

In this verse, a man who lacks self-control is a person like a city whose walls are broken down. It means an unfortified state that the enemy can attack anytime. It is a kind of state where the devil can work as much as he likes.

"Above all else, guard your heart, for it is wellspring of life" (Proverbs 4:23).

To live or die depends upon how we manage our thoughts.

When I was a senior in high school, I went a totally different way in my life because of just one thought. At that time, my family's financial situation gave me almost no hope that I could go to a college. In fact, to give up going to college was not the only issue. We were in a bad living situation because our debt was growing

185

everyday with interest. The only thing I could hold on to in the situation was God. Whenever the extremely difficult situations depressed me during my youth, I climbed up on a mountain and cried out to the Lord. And then I used to come back home with answers from God. It was also a result of good thinking in a crucial moment. What would have happened in my life if I went a bad way instead of going to the mountain to pray in the crucial moment? When the situation was harder, I thought to seek the Lord even more. With such a thought, the hopeless situation became the passageway of grace to experience God's grace.

No matter how hard I thought, it was almost impossible to go to a college, and I made a conclusion to myself. "The probability that I cannot go to a college is much higher. If it is true, my grade in the senior year of high school will be the last grade as the capability in my life. Then, I need to study even harder."

I grew up with the determination to live for Christ throughout my whole life. But if I could not study any further, I thought I could please God preparing myself by studying much harder during the time that was left. With this idea, I could not help but to always study very seriously.

But even before I took my entrance exam, a strange thing happened: I was chosen as an honor student to receive a full scholarship to a university. It was more than enough. I bought whatever I needed like the school uniform, shoes, a watch, books, and so on. I had only one good thought: God fulfilled my needs over flowingly and led me to abundance.

What would have happened if I was caught up with negative thoughts and just gave up studying? At that time, I learned that even in desperate situations, if one has hopeful thoughts repeatedly, then God plants the seeds of blessings on the ground of good thinking. I was so happy with the thought of becoming a person who plants the seeds of hope in the future.

Thus, thoughts work as a strong motive to bring blessings or curses. So Satan strikes our hearts and minds with all kinds of strategies to occupy our thoughts. There is no way to stop him without being filled with the Holy Spirit.

Piety Breaks Down the Strategies of Satan

As it is shown in the Bible, the fall of man resulted from the thoughts of human hearts. Look at the times of Noah. The people at that time were evil in every thought and plan of their hearts.

> "The LORD saw how great man's wicked-
> ness on the earth had become, and that
> every inclination of the thoughts of his
> heart was only evil all the time. The LORD
> was grieved that he had made man on the
> earth, and his heart was filled with pain"
> (Genesis 6:5–6).

The corruption of man is revealed in his thoughts of the heart. There will be no hope for mankind if anyone thinks of only sinful and dirty thoughts day and night and if he plans only evil. If his thoughts are corrupt, it means everything is corrupt. When humans reached this level during Noah's time, God decided to destroy mankind. This shows how much God considers our thinking and plans in our hearts significantly. Jesus also spoke about the importance of the state of our heart in the following verse. "A good man brings good things out of the good stored up in him, and an evil man brings evil things out of the evil stored up in him" (Matthew 12:35). This verse implies that good or evil thoughts are accumulated in the storehouse of our hearts. A person who has a larger collection of good thoughts shows goodness in his or her words and behaviors, but the one who is full of evil words and thoughts emanates the evil words and behaviors.

If there is a place where Satan's attacks are concentrated the most in order to control the important thoughts of our heart, it is our eyes. What we see determines the state of our hearts decisively.

The world we live in has been changing to a more visual world. That means that bigger temptations stimulate us. Whenever we wake up, there are temptations. In this world, it is almost impossible for us to live any longer without televisions, cell phones, and computers. How much have we actually been accepting greed, obscenity, competition, and secular worldviews indiscriminately? In order to not sin, the world today became a better place for the blind.

Take a look at David. He committed a serious sin through what he saw with his eyes. David loved God truly. He also received God's grace abundantly. But how can we understand such a person who committed this obscene sin? The moment when he saw Bathsheba taking a bath with nothing on in the middle of the day, he was caught by the obscenity. The scene did not leave from his mind.

We have to understand the facts. In a spiritual battle, Satan attacks our thoughts concentrically through our eyes. He makes us meditate the evil thoughts repeatedly. This is like putting garbage into our heads continually. If our minds are filled with trash again and again, what happens? The maggots and mice will infest it. The evil spirits will work. That is the reason why David committed the sin. What would have happened if he had talked like this, when he saw the naked body of Bathsheba?

"Oh, no, see the woman! How can she take a bath in the middle of the day so that everyone is able to see? How does she have such a behavior, knowing that men can watch her? Men, can you see the woman? Go and punish her! Tell her, if she does it again, I will strike her!"

If he attacked in this way, he would not have sinned. But the moment he saw her, instead of attacking, he was captivated by her. The mind to hold her in his arms preceded the heart to hate the sin of obscenity.

Satan is a being who has such a strong pride. So, if we fight against him strongly, then he will leave from us. If we hate him, Satan cannot keep coming around us. If we resist him in the name of Jesus, Satan will flee from us.

However, surprisingly, many people like Satan. They want to live with him. That's the problem. There are few who cut off the sweetness of sin boldly and take the life to live with the Holy Spirit as the best pleasure.

"Submit yourselves, then, to God. Resist the devil, and he will flee from you" (James 4:7).

It is okay if we always live according to this Word. Declare it when sin comes into your lives.

"I dislike you. I hate you. Get away from me, Satan."

But when David looked at the woman, he enjoyed the sinful thoughts about her. For an instant, he enjoyed the sinful thoughts, the trash of obscenity occurred, and eventually his heart was whirled by the wastes of lust. From that moment, he lost his rationality. He did not overcome his own will. David ordered Bathsheba to be called up and even had her husband killed indirectly. It did not take long for this crime to happen. Even David who had a godly life committed a great sin because he did not control his eyes.

Christians must control their eyes well. Pastors especially are to control their eyes very well. If your eyes are focused on television, computers, lustful magazines, nice cars, and houses when you have to pray for your members beside riversides of grace, meditating on God's words and saturating your thirsty spirits with God's grace, your spirits will be unconsciously filled with arrogance, greed, laziness, vanity, and tricks instead of being filled by grace. When you preach with that kind of spiritual state, although it is the same sermon, you cannot challenge anyone at all. How can a pastor possibly share God's grace when the Holy Spirit of the Lord God is sighing out of grief towards him? Just as dry skies do not give rain, grace cannot flow out when the pastor's heart is not filled with God's grace.

Because of that, pastors should be wiser in their hobbies and spare time. If the hobby could be a stumbling block in any way, it is better to decide not to have it. Good hobbies can give vitality to pastors, but if the hobbies hinder us from having a godly life, we must become such people who throw them away firmly because throwing them away become blessings to us eventually.

One pastor who liked soccer games too much was sitting at the church to watch a soccer game with the elders. It was about time for the afternoon service, but the pastor was not able to stop watching the game. He panicked, saying, "The game must finish as soon as possible for the service . . ." How much would church members deplore a pastor like him?

In another incident, one elder had a hard time because he was not able to stop watching pornographic videos. He was usually living in God's grace, but whenever he was away on business trips or was in some places by himself, he had a bad habit of watching pornography. Although he did not commit sins like lying or stealing, this brought a pleasure from which he could not resist. In the meantime, he realized some strange things were happening. Every time he tried to watch pornography at a hotel, one of his family members would get very sick. When he received a call regarding his son having a seizure or his wife having sudden sharp pains in her stomach, he thought all of this was a mere coincidence. But on the other side, he wondered if God was punishing his family because he had been watching the obscene videos. Wondering about this idea, he decided to test one thing intentionally. He called and checked in advance if anyone was sick in the family and watched a video comfortably. After that, he called his family again. He was surprised to find that an ambulance had been called to his house because one of his family members got sick suddenly at the very same time he turned on the video. It was proof of God's wrath.

The habits of a human being are difficult to heal in a day. The elder continued to watch pornographic videos again. In doing so, a contract that had been near completion dissipated all of a sudden. Finally, he realized God's sign clearly, and he asked for God's forgiveness, repenting of his sin in tears. He said God told him at that time, "Do you know how much I was grieving when you enjoyed watching those obscene movies? Aren't you my holy bride?"

It is true. We all are holy brides of the Lord. How we live as His brides can make God, our bridegroom, either be in grief or have a bright smile.

If we truly love our God, we should give our eyes to see, our hands to use, and our feet to Him totally. Meditating on the Word and praying to the Lord should be our pleasure, and taking care of the church members should be our repose. That is the life of people who belong to Heaven.

Once, I was touched deeply by a story about a man who committed all of his life to campus ministry. In the book he said, "I am much more pleased with sharing God's Word, evangelizing people, and ministering on a campus than soaking my feet in the cool sea. It is my spiritual rest."

There will be times when we need to take a full rest. In those times, we need to take enough time for rest. It is a shortcut to do our ministry more effectively. Resting can be considered part of our ministry.

However, we must not sin for the rest of the time. Also, when we still have the energy to run for our ministry, we must have a burning passion toward God's Kingdom and His Righteousness, feeling the ministry itself as rest. Such life is only possible when we are living a godly life. If a godly life is settled in our daily life, the level of life will be changed. The level of ministry will also be different. The ministerial field becomes the field of grace and power because the Holy Spirit takes care of all things. It is a field where the Holy Spirit can work fully.

CHAPTER 9

Family: When Your Family Smiles, Your Ministry Will Smile As Well

You Must Feel Heaven at Home

Everyone lives with a wish. But there is a common point among all wishes. It is a wish to experience heaven while we are living here on earth. Besides Christians who believe in the reality of heaven, even people who do not believe in the presence of heaven like to live in a place like heaven.

So what is heaven like? According to the Scriptures, heaven is a place of eternal happiness. It is a place where there is no death, no sorrow, no pain, no suffering, no aging, and no sickness. The Scripture also says that in heaven there is no hatred, no envy, and no fighting, but instead, it overflows with love and joy. Thus, heaven must be a totally different place than the world that we live in now. In this world, we are constantly surrounded by sorrow, suffering, death, and grief. We get older and sicker, and we also experience hatred, dissension, and jealousy.

That is the reason we need Jesus. Until we believe in Jesus, accept him as our Savior and Lord, and are born again by the Holy Spirit, we cannot experience heaven in this world. It is the only way to heaven. "I tell you the truth, whoever hears my word and believes him who sent me has eternal life and will not be condemned; he has crossed over from death to life" (John 5:24).

This means whoever believes in Jesus will have eternal life and blessings in heaven. It also means that if you believe in Him and become a child of God, you can experience heaven here on earth, although you have not entered heaven yet. When Jesus is in our hearts, you can experience heaven whether you live in a hut or in a royal palace; everywhere can be heaven.

God built up the family as a model of heaven and allowed us to experience the joy of heaven while we are living in this world. That is why pastors serve in their ministry with all their energy. They try to find the answer day in and day out to the question, "How can we help the congregation experience the joy of heaven in the church?"

Embracing the church members, pastors pray for them and try to wipe away their tears. As a result, many people come to church exhausted, and they experience being strengthened again by meeting the Lord in church. Although it is not perfect, such things happen that people experience the joys and hopes of heaven in the church.

However, one very strange issue is that many pastors do not work as hard to make heaven in their households as they work to make heaven in their churches. There are many pastor couples that smile at church but cry at home. They repent at church, saying, "It's my fault," but they raise their complaining voices up at home, saying, "It is your fault!" Why does this happen? The answer is because they have missed the ministry field where we have to work the most—at home.

I read about one family's description of home. The home is the place where a crying baby and mother's lullaby make a beautiful harmony. It is also where warm hearts and happy eyes meet each other. Home is where heartaches are mended, and happiness, joys, and sorrows are shared. It is a community where parents are respected and children are loved. Although there is little to eat, it is better than a palace. It is a place where money does not exercise much authority over people. Home is a school where the children first learn to love, learn what is right, learn to care for each other, and accept the care thankfully. It is the home, the most beautiful place.

If this describes a home, where else is there a place to embrace the joy of heaven than home on earth? But why can we hear the sounds of grief and lamentation instead of joy from so many families? If a pastor's home does not reflect the model of heaven, although the sound of heaven can be heard at church, a pastor's heart will only be filled by sorrows and pains. To a pastor, the family is the first given place to take rest and to do ministry. If there is devastation, then there is no choice but for the pastor's heart and soul to become dry and barren.

Therefore, a pastor's family should be happy. There are many helpers at church, but if there is no co-work with a pastor's wife at home, the ministry cannot be stable. In that situation, although the pastor preaches love, eventually his shouting will be "a resounding gong or a clanging cymbal."

The pastor, therefore, truly must be a man of practice at home. If he preaches the Lordship of the Holy Spirit at church but tries to dominate at home, and if he preaches to serve first at church but commands family members only to serve, what a hypocritical life like "whitewashed tombs" this is!

The Lord wants us to learn through our family what a true partnership is, what love is, what acceptance is, what the meaning to treat others as we do to the Lord is, what long patience is, and what dedication is. That is why we cannot avoid discussing the "home" because it is the place that our naked body is exposed the most genuinely.

The Happiness Index of Family Increases as Much as You Are Prepared

Some time ago, I started doing the dishes that my wife usually did because she is busier than I am in some ways. I used to tell her, "You'll be used by God greatly," and it really became true. I do not have a problem with this because I can use the electronic rice cooker when I need to cook rice. And I can eat the side dishes from the refrigerator whenever I need them because there are many side dishes. Therefore, one day I declared to my wife, "Honey! Since God has given you so many precious works to do, I feel it is a waste of time for you to spend time making food for me. So you are now free from the kitchen! You don't need to cook, and you don't need to make any side dishes for me anymore. I promise I won't complain about this ever. Be free!"

So I started cooking, and actually, she even loves my cooking! One day she said that the *Kimchi Chigye* that I made was delicious, and she took it to a meeting with other pastors' wives and shared it with them.

The expression of our love and affection for each other is not less than that of young couples. When she is doing the dishes, I go behind her and hold her in my arms. Sometimes I share about such actions during my sermons because by opening my family story, I want to emphasize how much the happiness of family in the life of saints is crucial. When I lead a couple's seminar, I even train the couples to be more familiar in expressing their affection to one another. Since I have received joy and energy through my family, I expect the families in our church to experience them as well.

However, our happiness index was not high from the beginning. We obtained the fruits through many mistakes, trials, and errors. I was not aware that for the happiness of a family, first, God's grace must be poured into our family, and then, both husband and wife must try hard and do their best. I really did not recognize that it was the home where we serve according to God's Word and that the home is the place where the pastor's living faith is proved.

I had never learned, nor was I interested in what a husband meant to his wife and how two different people meet to make one family and to live together. I was just a man who was not ready at all, but took a sweet, young woman into marriage. I am sure that I put her through much distress and hardship. I had prepared hard for pastoral ministry from very early on, but there was no preparation for family in my journey.

More than anything, I wanted to live my life only according to God's will. I had actually prepared my heart to serve God. Maybe this was the reason why I was so hesitant about marriage. If God wanted me to go to Africa or ordered me to go to an isolated island, my heart was ready to obey that calling, so I felt it would be less stressful to live by myself like the apostle Paul. I felt that if I was not living by myself would hinder me from leaving for any place at any time, so I put off marriage over and over. If I had to marry, I wanted a woman who grew up poor and with many hardships, a woman who knew only the Lord seeking her hope only in prayers. I also wanted a woman who graduated only from elementary school so that she would obey her husband's words completely, considering her husband just as heaven.

When it came near the time of my ordination, the presbytery said that they could not ordain an unmarried man, so I had no choice but to marry someone as soon as possible. Around that time, some professors and people around me started to recommend several precious ladies for me. Strangely, however, my heart was not moved at all. Just at that moment, one of the female evangelists showed me a picture of a woman—now my wife—and asked what I thought of her. She was the daughter of an elder in the church. "Well, she is okay! Well . . . !" I said.

Only that one word changed my life and my wife's life. Whenever people showed me just pictures, I always said, "I don't think I'm ready to meet somebody yet," but I don't know why I said, "Okay" at that time. As soon as my words were expressed, the wedding plans progressed with lightning speed.

At the moment, I was an associate pastor at Sinhyun Church, and my wife was a college student. She was also one of the elder's beloved daughters in the church. The female evangelist told the elder about my response. His family was pleased with me and gave me a suggestion:

"Because he's a pastor, we'd better rush the engagement before any weird rumors get started."

Just like that, our wedding preparation progressed. How preposterous was it for her to be engaged and married to me, not by her will, but by her father's forced will? She later told me that she cried for days saying that this was not fair, but because she was brought up to obey her father, she gave up on protesting. Without any preparation in her heart, she had a wedding ceremony with a man who was even a pastor. Our sudden engagement was the big talk of the church at that time. Even the senior pastor and his wife were shocked by the news that they said they were not able to sleep.

Everyone was very surprised, but no one was more shocked than my wife and I. We married first without any preparation for marriage. It was obvious that many problems were waiting between us, dashing this way and rushing that.

My Wife Also Had Suffering in Her Heart

After the wedding ceremony, I realized that we were too different. I grew up poor, but she grew up in a wealthy family. I was from Seoul, but her family was originally from North Korea. I am introverted and quiet, but she is outgoing with a loud voice. I liked spicy food, but she liked mild food. I was gentle and very careful in everything, while my wife was lively and flighty in everything.

Oh, how could we be so different? I should have accepted and understood her bright personality as lovely and beautiful as she was. But at that time, I thought, "I'm in such big trouble." Was it because of my traditional patriarchal mindset or was it a feeling of self-accusation? Just after marriage, I was obsessed with the idea that, "I have to make the woman obey me totally in a week."

I decided not to praise her in any way, and not to say "beautiful," "delicious," or "well done." Then she would not be boisterous. And I acted in this way. Therefore, how embarrassed and lonely was my wife during that time? When she went to church, she served and loved church members with all her heart. But whenever she came back home, she never had any praising words from her husband. How sad she must have been during that time! How heartbroken she must have been looking at her husband who shuts his mouth when he is upset with something! Many years later, she told me that there were times when I did not say a word for up to two weeks at a time. My wife married me just following her father's will, "the most valuable life was only to work for the Lord," trusting only one thing that I was a man of faith. But as for a young wife, each day must have been like hell.

All this happened because I didn't know how to embrace and love this woman who was very different from me. I knew how to care for the flock of sheep that God had given me, but I did not know how to love my one and only spouse. Of course, I had a loving heart and I liked her, but I did not know how to express my feelings towards her. I didn't even ask her to prepare a meal for me. When she cooked, I ate, and when she didn't, I didn't eat. When I visited church members' homes as a pastor, I was fed very well, so it didn't matter to me to skip a meal at home. My heart was completely filled with only the ministry. I used to pray passionately at dawn prayer meeting early in the morning. After dawn prayer meeting, I visited church members' homes all day long and came back home late in the evening. I simply repeated this life every day. I didn't even know that I was doing something wrong. I thought I was doing well since I lived serving God so faithfully. I did not even notice that my wife's face was getting darker and was gradually losing her vivid character.

Whenever my wife looks back upon those days, she expresses her feelings with the words that she just wanted to die. She said she tried to leave a note and run away far from me, but she gave up the plan. One occasion, she said, she threw herself on God's mercy, praying and fasting for seventeen days. Thankfully, God always responded to her in that situation, saying, "Your husband is a servant of God, so you should live obeying him." If God had not spoken to her that way, I would have lived as a single man from very early on until now.

In spite of her situation, this cold-hearted husband did not even know that his wife was praying and fasting. Instead, I was glad in my mind, understanding she was trying to obey my will. Actually, since she received the answer from God, she was becoming noticeably a more obedient wife. Looking back, I can see that she had a much more mature and wide faith than I. She strived to resolve all the problems before the Lord as a person who was brought up in the faith. Even when she was hurting inside, she never stopped praying for her husband and children, and she tried to do her best in order to build up "the home of faith."

Since I was such a simple-minded person who was not able to see my wife's inner mind, watching over my wife, I thought, "Everything is going well." I had always lived in poverty, embracing all the burdens in my home. But because of the household that my wife had brought, I was able to sleep with a nice quilt and live a more comfortable life. I was so comfortable because my wife gave birth and raised my children so well by herself, and she always prepared meals for me. Particularly, my wife supported me in prayer whenever I prepared a sermon. While I prepared the sermon, she went to another room and prayed for a couple of hours for me. After I finished my manuscript for the sermon, she would rewrite it on another paper with her beautiful handwriting so that it would be easier to read when I preached. After we had children, she also led them to support me in prayers together. Sometimes my children would gather together, praise God, and pray for me when their mother was not with them. When I saw this scene, I would be in tears.

When we raised our children, if our babies woke up and cried in the early morning, she quickly would take them out of the room, calm them, and then return to the room. She knew and worried for her husband to sleep well for the dawn prayer meetings, so she raised two children like that. I realized such facts a long time later. I did not know that she woke during the night to feed our babies or take our crying babies out of the room to soothe them. In short, I was very blessed to be married to such a good wife.

As for her, however, it seemed that she had only troubles after she got married. She had been well off since she was young, but after she married a poor pastor, she had to do much housework: laundry, cleaning, errands for me, and she also went through pregnancy and labor alone. I cannot imagine how hard it was for my wife.

But I never mollified my wife's heart even once.

That is a pitfall of a pastor's family. I should have asked her to be involved with prayers, asking, "I have such and such a thing and I need your prayer," and let her share the joy of achievement with me in my ministry. However, I always left her out. It is a husband's duty to be a friend to his wife and to listen to her carefully, especially the stories inside of her that she cannot say to anyone. However, I did not say anything to her even about my story.

I did not know the true meaning of working together at that time. Taking care of our sheep together, sharing testimonies together, praying together and being joyful—it is the ministry of "working together." In the house, although a wife raises the children alone all day long, she should ask for her husband's help when he comes home from his work. "Our children behaved like this today. What should I do? I think I need your guidance." Having communication like this and gathering the wisdom for raising children together should be a posture as parents to have a beautiful partnership. If a wife takes all the responsibility for the children without any discussion with her husband and enjoys the accomplishments alone, how big is the sense of loss and loneliness for the husband!

It is the same in the ministerial field. The ministerial field becomes the healthiest pastoral field through working together between husband and wife. I did not know that. I considered her as a woman who just cooked and looked after children. I lived forgetting that she was the closest friend to work together with me and my only lover in this world.

If I were a woman, could I have tolerated this place willingly? If I were forced to live like that, I would have never been married. Nonetheless, women marry even though they know what their place could be, accepting such hardships willingly. Why is this so? Maybe, it is because they have an expectation to be loved by their husbands. Women were created to feel happiness in love from their husbands, and men were created to feel comfort from the respect given by their wives. So the scripture orders to the husbands, "Love your wife." The scripture determines the role and responsibility of the husbands is to love their wife unto death.

However, I did not live according to these words. And what was the result? In the end, the loss must belong to the husband. Because I had not taken her in my arms, there was no opportunity to have delicious meals from my wife. She seemed to have lost her interest in cooking, and eventually she only put some red pepper paste and dried anchovies on the table for dinner with some rice. But I was not moved by that. Originally I was raised in poor conditions, so there was no reason not to have food, even if the dried anchovies were all for dinner. Due to such a husband, my wife was losing her joy in the housework. There was neither laughter nor joy in my home. It was always quiet and solemn like a funeral home. There was no one to welcome me and look at me with respect in my home. In the end, the husband who did not embrace his wife with love brought loss onto himself because I did not love her in the way I should have, and there was no love to be returned.

Love Is Concern

The first three years of my married life passed by just like that. One day, suddenly I had a question. "Is there anything wrong with the way I was thinking?" Once this thought entered into my heart, I, such a simple man, decided my plan. "Well, then I will change my plans now."

That very night I made the decision and talked to my wife, patting her shoulders. It was the first time since I married her.

"Are you tired? How was your day today, honey?"

It was the first time my wife had ever heard a tender voice from me in three years of marriage. Her face brightened up all of a sudden. That evening, the dinner menu was changed. Unlike every other day when dinner was only red pepper paste and dried anchovies, she borrowed some young radish Kimchi from a neighbor in a hurry and set it on the table. When I tasted it, it was so sour that I could hardly eat it. But I did not complain.

"Honey, this Kimchi is the best I've ever had."

After dinner, I said to her one more word. "I enjoyed the meal. Thank you for your hard work!" The very next day, I did not have any idea where she gathered all that strength, but she went to the market bringing our two kids together and bought some nice cabbage to make fresh kimchi and a delicious fish for us to eat. She also bought some linen and made a curtain for the window, bought flowers to put in the corner of the room, and started to make some clothes for the children. She was such a lovely and womanly lady. Because she was the woman who had such a vivid energy, she put the vitality everywhere in the house. Receiving the love and praise, her merit that had been hidden was brought out simultaneously.

When I gave my love to her as her husband, she gave me back several times more of her love and service. The atmosphere of my house completely changed. At this moment, I said to my wife, "Honey, Shakespeare said that life is a play. In this family where you and I are the main characters, let us make this play a comedy, not a tragedy from now on. Then we will enjoy it and our audiences will enjoy it as well."

She made a pinky promise with my suggestion. My two daughters were in another room at that moment, so I held my wife tightly and said, "Honey, I've never seen a woman as beautiful as you. The more I see you, the more I love you!"

Then, my wife said to me back soon, "I like you even if I see your back side."

Although we knew that was like a play, we continued to praise each other in order to keep the promise we made just before. How fun this was! After that incident, the flower of laughter bloomed in our family. Ever since we made a paradigm shift from no interest to full interest and from no response to compliments, our play turned from a tragedy to comedy. Our love as a couple always concluded each day with a happy ending.

Once I hugged my wife from behind when she was washing the dishes. Suddenly she leaned back on me with her stout body, being totally relaxed. I tried not to fall down, gathering energy on my legs. She asked me with a smile, "Honey, I'm fat, right?"

"No, you're too slim."

She didn't need to ask me anymore because my answer was always the same: "You're beautiful, you're slim, and you're blessed."

I was a man who knew nothing about women. Many pastors seem to have difficulty in their homes because they do not know much about women either. Sometimes they often leave their family behind because they are unaware of the truth that they must build their family up with all their heart just as they do the pastoral ministry.

We therefore need to prepare and study well for the family. Ministers must do more. Because a pastor's family is open to the members, the influence is great. That is why a pastor's family should be built more preciously. For that, pastors need to study about women.

> "Husbands, in the same way be considerate as you live with your wives, and treat them with respect as the weaker partner and as heirs with you of the gracious gift of life, so that nothing will hinder your prayers" (1 Peter 3:7).

In this verse, Peter the Apostle tells us to live with wives together according to knowledge. That means if you want to make your wife happy, you should have knowledge about what she wants and what she doesn't want. Why do we have to work hard to learn about women? Because a wife is the person who will inherit the grace of life with you together, she is the most precious one—more than anyone. It is the wife that a husband should treat as the most precious one. A woman feels the worth of being when her husband treats her as the most precious one. When husbands consider their wives as the most precious ones, the unlimited talents and abilities that God has given to them can be manifested fully. On the other hand, if husbands do not treat their wives preciously, wives lose their strength and desire of the heart, like a wilting flower. Expecting only the love from her husband, a wife will go through all difficulties since she has been married. If a husband does not give his love, the wife will wither like flowers that have not been receiving sunlight.

What is it to consider preciously? It is to understand your wife's efforts and to know your wife's mind. It is to know and fulfill her needs.

"Honey, are you okay? Are you tired?

"Honey, you need to rest. Take a rest for a week and do nothing. I'll take care of everything for a week. You just take a vacation for a week."

"Honey, I can't do anything without you. I can only work this ministry this much because you give me your advice and pray for me. You are the blessing in our family."

It is no use just shouting out to the congregation from the pulpit. "You're born to be worthy just from the moment when you believe in Jesus Christ!" If a pastor does not build his wife as the most precious one at home, the pastor's pulpit cannot be a fountain of true forgiveness and a fountain of acceptance and respect. Pastors preach the Gospel and expect changes in the lives of the church members, but God may want a minister's home to be changed first according to His Word.

For changes with the families, God seriously wants to see pastors living by His Word first.

If Your Family Smiles, the Pastoral Ministry Smiles as Well

When I speak about these things, most husbands might reply, "Because I am a human being, I want to take a rest even at home. Do I have to read my wife's face even at home, because I worked all day long outside, reading other people's faces?"

The reason these questions are asked is that they really have not experienced yet how much of a great joy and vitality there is to loving their wives. It is because they do not know that reducing the wife's labors and encouraging the wife are not just "a certain great work," it is "the rest."

Pastors should not recognize the Scripture reading and prayers simply as a duty that they must perform. If they think so, the ministry of Scripture reading and prayers becomes a heavy burden, and you are not able to receive the power of the Holy Spirit. When we recognize scripture reading and prayers as "breathing," when we live with the confessions that "the time for prayer is the most joyful," and "the first day I received the Word, it was really joyful and happy," the power of God will be given every day. If you can "breath with the Lord and live with God" as your life style, then you do not need to receive the power of pastoral ministry separately because the lifestyle itself becomes the power, and it will appear.

In the same way, if a husband thinks that to love his wife is hard work, the power of love cannot be manifested in the home. Loving, encouraging, and helping your wife is not a ministry, but a root of joy. Change your thoughts! If you change just one thought, then you do not have to work extra to make your home as heaven. It becomes heaven.

I have traveled all over the world to lead revival rallies. During these times, I especially try to spend time building up missionary wives because I can see their sorrow and sufferings in these families.

When I saw the faces of missionary wives that were depressed and thinking about suicide, my heart broke. Because of that, when I went for revival rallies, I actually led a healing seminar for the missionary couples instead of a revival rally from time to time.

It happened in a mission field one time. When I met a missionary couple, the pastor seemed to be filled abundantly with the Holy Spirit, but the wife's face looked downcast. In my mind a warning bell rang. I felt God had called me to this rally to recover her more so than any others. I struggled to find some ways that I could help her.

After the rally was over, there was a small party, surprisingly, at the missionary's home. It was a potluck party where each family brought a dish. At the party, I addressed the following message to everyone.

"Everyone, it is very good that you all are gathering together for fellowship and sharing love in this way. However, we must remember one thing. When we share food like this, in fact, there is a great sacrifice of one person for this fellowship. Who is the missionary wife? The missionary wife is a woman too. A woman needs her own personal room. I say the space where she can sleep pulling her bedclothes over her head whenever she is exhausted. She needs a private room where she can leave everything unorganized and where she can breathe by herself. But when I came here, I was utterly surprised. There is no space for her at all. There is no space for the missionary wife to use alone. When I saw her face, she seems like she's ready to collapse. I feel like everyone here needs to help her get such a room or move the family to another house. What do you think?"

In fact, I usually don't like preaching in revival rallies, saying the following words intentionally, "Serve your pastor. Serve in this way." But at that time, I thought it was quite urgent. As a matter of fact, she was becoming a sacrifice by extremely heavy works. Her husband was able to take care of the sheep, but he could not see that his wife was at the point of falling. There were not only church members who visited the missionary's house. The missionary family was accepting some troubled children of other Korean pastors as well. Therefore, the missionary wife needed to take care of many people. When some children made problems, it was she who worried. Thus, she was exhausted, but no one cared for her.

I encouraged the pastor.

"You may find your life worth living and have encouragements from others while you are working for the Lord outside the home. But how about your wife? Everyone is in and out of your house all the time, and it is she who takes care of your children. Plus, she is looking after all of these children . . . it is she, not you, who takes care of all these things! If you have decided to bring in children and asked your wife to take care of them according to your will, then you must help her out. Can't you see that she has no place to even breathe for a few minutes without being interrupted?"

Then, his wife started to cry. Once she started to cry, she didn't stop for a long time. It was a cry of sadness and sorrow. Soon, her tears were contagious to others; all the church members in the room started crying with her, and the crying continued through the night. A few years later when I met the family again, I could see that the wife had been changed greatly like a different person.

I do not know if it might be impudent; however, I have been doing this as if it is a significant mission for me. When I see the family of the Lord's servants collapsing, I can't stop thinking to find some ways to restore them. When a healthy family is established, the pastoral ministry will stand healthy for a long time.

The Fountain of Happiness of Family Is Faith!

Home is the starting point and the destination of pastoral ministry. When the sounds of love and happiness are overflowing in a pastor's household, a fountain of happiness also overflows in the church members' families. But happiness is not given freely. Neither is it given just by our efforts. No matter how much a husband loves his wife and no matter how hard a mother tries to help her child to be successful, they cannot achieve the fruits only through their efforts. For everything in a family to go well, God's grace should remain within the family.

What is *grace*? Grace is a free gift from God. Grace means being filled and completed by God's love even in the areas that we do not make an effort, we cannot estimate, or we cannot try with our own endeavors.

As we raise our children, we can soon realize that our children are not really raised by parents but by the grace of God. If parents do one thing for their children, God does one thousand or ten thousand things. A mother prepares a meal for her children, but God pours out thousands of blessings for the rice, the material for the meal, and then sends a sack of rice to our family. God provides early or late rain for the crops to become ripe, and He allows it to be cultivated by the farmers and finally sends them to our home through many different channels of distribution. A mother can only say to her children, "Watch out when you cross the street." But it is God who guards them from the pupil of His eye and manages the traffic in the midst of running cars in this dangerous world.

It is also God who always fills in their lives with challenges and grace. Thus, when God's grace remains in our family, our children can grow to maturity, and the couple can be united by love. All these facts mean that if we serve God, the Lord of family, well, our happiness can be guaranteed. Therefore, if we want to remain in God's grace, every member of the family must stand firm in the faith. We must live faithfully and have a vision for the family by faith. Living by faith is alpha and omega for the happiness of the family.

I earnestly believe that the power of a pastor's wife's prayer is equal to the power of the prayers of the entire congregation. To that extent, the prayer of the pastor's wife is the most earnest and sincerest of prayers. In that sense, the best type of wife for the pastor is the type of person who quietly prays for pastors without words, and the worst type as a pastor's wife will be the one who does not pray but criticizes.

I always praise my wife a lot. My wife also praises me a lot. When we do, we feel very thankful for each other. However, when we feel the happiest is also the time praying for each other. The moment when my wife and I are together for prayer, I feel it is more graceful than any Revival Rallies and special meetings. At that time, we experience heaven here on earth. At that time, we can experience the highest jubilation at home. Many people of this world do not understand and question this experience.

"Are you really happy living that way?"
I respond to them in positive affirmation.
"Live like me! If you do, you will experience that heaven will be moved into your home."

In prayers, a husband and wife wipe each other's tears, sleep together with the same covers, talk about the Lordship of the Lord, and share their difficulties with each other. "Let us solve this problem with prayers. Let's wonder: how God would work for this?"

At that moment, heaven is experienced in our lives on the earth. Thus, when everyone in the family has a clear lifestyle to live with faith, the family will receive abundant blessings sooner or later. From God's side, it is not difficult to give us His blessings. However, it is difficult for us to live faithfully in His Word. If we live to obey His Word, if our household receives God as the Lord according to the Word, God will take care of everything and bless us.

> "Do not let this Book of the Law depart from your mouth; meditate on it day and night, so that you may be careful to do everything written in it. Then you will be prosperous and successful" (Joshua 1:8).

This is God's heart. God considers carefully how to bless families. The problem is that the Lord's servants' families do not love completely according to God's Word, do not believe fully and do not serve faithfully according to His Word.

Surely, there may be a time when a sacrifice of family is required inevitably. There may also be a time of trouble. Nevertheless, if you live according to God's Word even in the situation, eventually God will bless you abundantly.

Even now, there is something that I am very sorry about toward my second daughter. My three children were born with gentle characters and were never troublemakers. God formed good characters in my children and raised them directly holding their hands. They were so good. Around the time they were one year old, they could worship by themselves at Sunday service, sitting in the first row during the entire worship. They would sit all alone and fall asleep during the service because their mother had to serve in the choir and their father had to preach from the pulpit. They all grew up as really good kids in that way.

However, there was one time I spanked my second child when she was about four years old. When my wife and I were getting ready to do a home visitation, my second child started whining because she did not want to be away from us. We explained as much as she could understand. "Mommy and daddy must have visitation today. Stay home just for a while."

However, she still cried. We could not delay any longer so we left the house with her crying still. We felt terrible, but we could not cancel the visitation.

Our daughter came running after mom and dad. I took her into the house and gave her a few spanks. Dad's punishments are scary for children. I hardly ever punished my children, so once I picked up a paddle, they were very. I went to the visitation leaving behind the scared child. Then, I forgot about the whole incident.

A few years ago, my second daughter, who was studying in the United States, had an opportunity to talk with my wife. My wife said that while she was talking, she said while crying, "Mom, I don't know why my tears fall whenever I recall that moment. I understand Dad and in that situation he did the right thing, but tears fall down."

Ah, my heart was really broken when I heard that conversation. The next time I saw my daughter, I asked sincerely for her forgiveness. Whenever I had to punish my children, I always held them tightly in my arms afterwards. That was the kind of father I was. However, in this one instance, I not only spanked my daughter but also left her without any hug.

"Please forgive me. I love you so much."

After that, believing that God healed even the root of that scar inside my daughter's heart, I am living as a father who embraces my children and prays for them more and more.

Like this, every family goes through trial and error. Sometimes painful marks have been left clearly. Even so, from now on, if you love according to God's Word and if you live with faith according to God's Word, then I believe that God will bless the family of the Lord abundantly. Even today, God wants to bless us truly and abundantly.

The following is written by Pastor Pildo Joung's wife, Shin-Shil Park.

A Spouse Is Not an Object to Depend on but to Serve

My husband and I are very different people. The tastes we have are also different. My husband likes people who are quiet and gentle. But I do not. Nevertheless, my husband loves me unconditionally. Maybe it is more than anyone can imagine. I learned many things from watching over my husband serving me as if I were Jesus.

My husband likes considering how our differences have become a passageway to complement each other's shortcomings. At first, of course, the fact that we were different was very hard to accept. If I said, "Ah," then my husband accepted that as "Uh," and if he said, "Ah," then I accepted that as "Uh." Therefore, the communication itself was not accomplished. Moreover, since it was almost like I was forced into marriage with my husband by my father, living with my husband was inevitably very hard.

All of these things, however, were parts of God's calling that He has disciplined me. My husband had been prepared to serve God thoroughly since he was young. He has lived always thinking of God alone, whether he sits down or stands up, and even if he lives or dies. His thought and his heart have been set upon God totally. He has lived a godly life as his habit.

On the other hand, I was not like him. Although I had been raised up in the faith, I grew up always under the protection of my parents without any particular hardships, so my inner faith was not so firm. The outside

216

was reckless and tomboyish, but inside was like a weak reed. It looked like a flower in a green house.

Because of that, my marriage with my husband was a discipline for me from the beginning. The first three years we lived with very much difficultly. Later, my husband repented for those years, but as for me, those three years were God's intentional calling period where He drew me nearer to Him. During that time, I went around looking for a church to pray in every day because I did not want to live any longer. I could not even share my mind with my parents who had raised me only in prayer. Eventually I just asked God, crying out, "Help me!" Since my husband was a chaplain at that time, I did not have any designated church to serve. Therefore, I had wandered around the town to find a church that was open. And if the church was closed, I even knocked on the locked doors to be let in so that I could pray. At that time, my husband looked like a person who completely devoted himself to the work of the Lord, even leaving his family behind. In this situation, all I could do was to depend on God desperately. The only object that I could rely on was the Lord.

Due to my husband's heartlessness, I could meet God very deeply for the three years. Through such desperate prayers, sometimes I could listen to God's voice and sometimes experience the presence of the Holy Spirit. Step by step, God brought me closer to Him in such ways.

After those three years, because my husband had been changed, my husband and I were able to sing a song of happiness; yet, how was it possible for everything to change through only one incident? I often got seriously sick because sometimes I was hurt by some words of my husband or other church members, or because sometimes I felt God's demands were too big for me. Yet, whenever I was suffering from several hardships, God granted me great testimonies of victory. Because of that, from some time ago, I came to be convinced that God had been leading me so that He would eventually give me the glorious and blessed crown. God was on my side, and He was my God. Therefore, I could not help but serve Him with all my body, heart, will, and sincerity. As time passed, I also was trying to live, seeking the godly life like my husband. My life had been changed little by little in that way. Most importantly, I was not retaining a lingering desire for money from being raised as a daughter of a wealthy family. If I had anything, I wanted to share it with others or to give it back to God. My husband was always watching me with such gratification in his eyes.

Yes. My husband was the person who always looked at me with gratification in his eyes. He never, even one time, forced me to pray or serve more. He waited for me until I had an active passion. I suppose it was probably when we were building the Education building. One day, I was touched by the Holy Spirit and said to my husband, "Honey, I decided to offer all your honoraria for the next four years to God!" When I said this, he gave me a clap for my dedication, saying, "Your face is red with your excitement!" From that time on, every single week, whenever he came back from leading the revival rallies, he gave all his honoraria to God.

I was able to enjoy my commitment to God and to rely on Him because of my husband. If my husband had forced me, I probably could not live following the way the Lord had guided. But my husband accepted and loved me just as I was. He encouraged and waited for me. In the waiting, I was able to experience meeting Jesus, the power of prayer, and the lordship of God only.

One night, I was very concerned about my husband's health because his condition looked serious. However, he would not slow down to consider his health at all. Instead, he stayed up until midnight or 1 A.M. to prepare for his broadcasting sermons. While I was praying in the other room as usual, that day, a great sadness somehow was driven into my mind. It was because of my fear that some bad thing could happen to my husband due to his declining physical situation.

At that moment, the Lord came to me and said, "Do you love me?"

After hearing His voice, I began to examine myself. I had to figure out why the Lord asked me such a question. Soon, the reality that I could not hide was exposed. What I truly feared was not "any bad thing that may happen to my husband" but, "how can I live if some bad things happened to my husband?" Just at that time, the Lord spoke to me again.

"Do you love me? Do you completely trust and love me?"

I prostrated myself before the Lord and started to cry.

"Lord, you are right. I did not trust you completely, but trusted provision and richness that came from my husband. Truly, I will love and trust only you from now on. I will hold onto only God in any situation."

Since that day, such confessions to the Lord continued several times. Especially when I was in the hospital from a car accident, God told me with a very quiet voice, "Get up and pray." He continued, "I planted you here." He said that it was neither my husband nor my father, but it was God who planted me here. Then, He told me about His plans for my husband and me. For that specific purpose, God said He united us together. At that moment, I realized that God had many things to do through us. I also realized that the husband and wife were the ones, who were called by God together, to help and encourage each other for the work.

Therefore, the husband and wife are the relationship to help in prayers and to encourage each other in love. The husband and wife are the ones who were called as helpers in order to accomplish the mission given to each other by God. Therefore, the husband and wife must help each other, but each one must try to do their best to rely on only God individually. It is the key to building a happy family. Husband and wife are not the objects to rely on, but to serve.

Since that time, I did not count on my husband as the object to rely on, although I love and respect my husband. I did not sigh, thinking only about how my husband talked to me or how church members talked about me. Instead, I only focused on the joy to live breathing with God, entrusting everything to the Holy Spirit. From that moment, I experienced the amazing peace and happiness that came into my home.

Until I came to that point, my husband has always considered me as a precious spouse and waited for me. In a race towards God, my husband never gave me a feeling that he had preceded me far away. Instead, he has watched me from a step behind.

Forty years of pastoral ministry! I have not helped my husband as a wife during that time. Rather, I have actually received his help. My husband has been helping me continuously so that I can be used by God.

CHAPTER 10

Church: The Church Will Win Victory For Sure

The Church Is the Only Hope for the World

There are many organizations, constitutions, and assemblies in the world. However, there is nothing more precious and special than the church. The church transcends time and space. From the time of the Apostles until now and to the saints who are in heaven or on the earth, we all belong to one Church. No organization, therefore, in the universe is bigger than the Church.

Especially, the Church is the most precious because the Lord built the Church through giving His life and shedding His blood. The Church is the place where the love of Christ is revealed the best. The Church, therefore, is the place where the Lord never turns His face away because the Church is the body of the Lord, and Jesus is the head of the Church (Colossians 1:18). No matter how much Satan, who is the ruler of the kingdom of the air attacks seriously, the Church is destined to prevail. We are fighting the fight already knowing the results.

Therefore, we need not worry for anything because we are the soldiers who are fighting the battles that we already have won. These soldiers just need to go and fight on the battleground for the already promised victory according to the Word of God. As we do, we must solve the problem of how to fight these battles.

> "Remain in me, as I will remain in you. No branch can bear fruit by itself; it must remain in the vine. Neither can you bear fruit unless you remain in me. 'I am the vine; you are the branches. If a man remains in me and I in him, he will bear much fruit; apart from me you can do nothing. If anyone does not remain in me, he is like a branch that is thrown away and withers; such branches are picked up, thrown into the fire and burned'" (John 15:4–6).

These words clearly show what we, as the living parts of the church, must do in order to win the promised victory. It is not to leave the Lord. In other words, the saints must not leave the Church. If one leaves the Church, he will wither away and die. Especially in these last days, the saints must live with the Church. Whether we live or die, we have to be connected to the Church, the body of the Lord.

We are the living parts of the Church that is the body of Christ. The parts must always move according to the direction given by the head. To be perfect, the Church must move according to the order of Jesus. If each part does not follow the directions from the head, it is clear evidence that the body is sick. If the hands or feet are paralyzed, or if the eyes cannot see, or if the ears cannot hear, these things happen when each part is not connected correctly to the nerve centers of the brain. This means that our body can play the role positively when the parts are moving together, following the direction of the head exactly. That is the Church. If there is this principle in the Church, God's promised victory must be given to us.

Since we are now living in the last days, the Church is our hope. We have to build the Church. We must let people know Jesus, the head of the body, being one body through the Church. This is the purpose why our Sooyoungro Church has been established. Being one body with the Lord, to accomplish the mission of the Lord, Sooyoungro Church was established about thirty years ago. To share the Gospel in Busan, in this country, and in the whole world, Sooyoungro Church was established on June 1, 1976.

I Want to Be a Pastor like a Reliable Eldest Brother

No matter what people say, the Church is the hope of the world. Because of this hope, there is a future in this country and in this land. Somehow Satan attacks to extinguish this light of hope like a roaring lion. In the center of the attack are the pastors. For this very reason, all the saints need to pray for pastors. To deprave one pastor, it has been told that the religious groups that serve Satan are praying to Satan with fasting. If a pastor falls, the church will be divided easily. It does not take long.

I have always kept this in my mind during my forty years of pastoral ministry. Probably because of this, my love and concern for pastors has been very special.

223

This is why I have so many things that I want to share, especially with pastors, looking back on the thirty-year history of Sooyoungro Church.

I love our church, especially our pastoral staff. I believe first that we pastors, must be one. The Bible teaches us well why we should be one.

> "As a prisoner for the Lord, then, I urge you to live a life worthy of the calling you have received. Be completely humble and gentle; be patient, bearing with one another in love. Make every effort to keep the unity of the Spirit through the bond of peace. There is one body and one Spirit, just as you were called to one hope when you were called; one Lord, one faith, one baptism; one God and Father of all, who is over all and through all and in all" (Ephesians 4:1–6).

These words tell us why we have to be one, and at the same time, how we can be one. To be one, we must be humble, gentle, patient, and accept each other in love, not trying to change others. When we accept other people as they are with love and humility, the church can be one by that time. I learned this through working together with my pastoral staff.

About ten years ago, as our church was growing, the number of associate pastors increased as well. However, according to increasing number of associate pastors, I became worried about their various levels of loyalty and passion. The problem was that no one person from the pastoral staff met my standards as a pastor. As a matter of fact, it is impossible for anyone to fit perfectly to my standards. Maybe it is not possible absolutely for anyone to fit one hundred percent to the standards that have been made by my own standard. But forgetting this fact, I worried very much, watching over the associate pastors. I thought, "How can they work for the task of the Lord if they are too lazy and idle?" I brought this to God and started to pray, insisting stubbornly.

"Lord, I cannot work with these pastors. Send me pastors who are ready to die with me for you as martyrs!"

Then the Lord answered, to my surprise, "Can you be such a pastor like the best reliable elder brother for the associate pastors so that they remember you through their lives?"

I was complaining to God that I could not work with these lazy and crooked pastors. But God was telling me to be their "best elder brother." With one word from the Lord, all my complaining and grumbling disappeared.

"If you say that, I will do it, Lord."

After this incident, I totally changed my patterns of working with the associate pastors at Sooyoungro Church. I gathered all associate pastors immediately and shared what had happened with them. And at the same time, I made an announcement clearly to all associate pastors in the meeting.

"From now on, all of you are the senior pastors. Therefore, don't worry about me and just work as you wish. I will never say anything about your ministry. If you make a mistake, I will be your shield and cover for you. Just don't sin and do not lead the congregation to heresy. Just work hard! Don't even make any reports to me. Let's decrease meetings as much as we can."

In God's eyes, they were all precious servants of the Lord. Even though they seemed lazy and no good to my own standards, they could be viewed totally different in God's eyes. If God sees their weaknesses, He will change them directly.

I complained to God that they did not meet my standards; therefore, I could not work with them, but God was asking me to accept them in love. He told me to embrace them like an elder brother. So from then on, I did not attend meetings or receive reports from them. Instead, I totally trusted them. By the way, it made the church one, and by becoming one, the church began to grow more rapidly. Since the faces of the associate pastors were filled with joy, the whole church began to fill with joy. Since they grew before the Lord, the church was growing naturally as well.

God wanted to teach me this fact: the church can be one when the pastors become one first, accepting each other in love and becoming one with humbleness and gentleness.

After that incident, as time passed from one year to two years, I gradually left more from the front line of the pastoral ministry at Sooyoungro Church. Because I have been involved in the pastoral ministry for forty years, my sense of the times is inevitably falling behind. Since I know this fact, I concentrate on the sermons and leave all the businesses and pastoral plans to the bright, young pastors. I am truly thankful for this fact. Even though I age year after year, Sooyoungro Church will keep the sense of the times due to the young and passionate pastors.

The Best Has Not Come Yet

I think God has answered most of my desires and hopes throughout my life. God gave me His grace and blessings abundantly. God allowed me to be a pastor as my dream when I was young, and He allowed me to see the church that has been growing every day differently. The wife of wisdom and virtue, the children who were raised well, my lovely saints of Sooyoungro Church who are so obedient to the Lord's work, and my co-workers of Sooyoungro Church who are working more powerfully and faithfully than me—when I think about these blessings from the Lord, I can say with confidence that I am the most blessed person! However, there is one thing that I am not satisfied with yet. Therefore, I pray in tears every dawn prayer time, watching over one promise of the Lord that has not come true yet: "Evangelization of Busan, evangelization of Korea, and evangelization of the world"

Since I was young, I have dreamed of the day when all the citizens of Korea would accept Christ as their Lord and Savior. I never lost the vision, "I will come true to evangelize Busan through my life," since I first started my ministry in Busan. Now, I am sixty-four years old, and there are six more years left for my retirement as the senior pastor of Sooyoungro Church. Still I believe that God will show me the best way to accomplish this vision sometime in the near future. Because I still believe that the best has not yet come, I cannot throw away the dream of evangelization of Busan, evangelization of Korea, and evangelization of the world.

To make this vision come true, our church has worked diligently from the very beginning to this day. This effort is natural to us. In a sense, the church exists for missions. Therefore, although the church is doing her best for missions, the church cannot boast anything about what they are doing. The apostle Paul tells us that in Corinthians: "Yet when I preach the Gospel, I cannot boast, for I am compelled to preach. Woe to me if I do not preach the Gospel" (1 Corinthians 9:16).

We are compelled to do missions work. If we do not, the Bible says that there will be a curse. Ezekiel supports the words clearly.

> "Son of man, I have made you a watchman for the house of Israel; so hear the word I speak and give them warning from me. When I say to a wicked man, 'You will surely die,' and you do not warn him or speak out to dissuade them from their evil ways in order to save his life, that wicked man will die for his sin, and I will hold you accountable for his blood. But if you do warn the wicked man and he does not turn from his wickedness or from his evil ways, he will die for his sin; but you will have saved yourself" (Ezekiel 3:17–19).

We, who have already been called, are the Lord's watchmen. Watchmen should live their lives proclaiming God's judgment for sin and God's blessing for righteousness and truth.

This proclamation work is the ministry of spreading the Gospel. We are responsible for spreading the Gospel as it is. Therefore, we must go to the ends of the earth with the Gospel, discipling all the nations so that the earth should be conquered by the Gospel. For this purpose, Sooyoungro Church has been praying, having a strategy to send 5,000 missionaries.

However, this vision cannot be realized with our own strength. It can only be accomplished through the work of the Holy Spirit. It is the real reason why we cannot boast, although we do our best for the missions work.

To let us know this fact, God always has used the insufficient people when He does His work. Who did

God use to save the people in the town of Sychar in Samaria? God used a shameful woman who had five husbands in the past and who lived with a man that was not her husband at that time. We cannot understand at all from our human perspective, but God is so eager to show us that everything is possible through the power of the Holy Spirit, not ours.

Still today, God seeks the weak people. Through them, God is developing His work through the Holy Spirit.

> "Brothers, think of what you were when you were called. Not many of you were wise by human standards; not many were influential; not many were of noble birth. But God chose the foolish things of the world to shame the wise; God chose the weak things of the world to shame the strong. He chose the lowly things of this world and the despised things—and the things that are not—to nullify the things that are, so that no one may boast before him" (1 Corinthians 1:26–29).

The ministry of mission to the world—God's great mission work—will be done through someone who has nothing to boast about in this world, someone whose hope is only in God's grace, someone who can work only after receiving God's power, and those who are insignificant. Through the world's history, it can be proven very clearly.

On January 2, 1956, a missionary, whose name was Piton, telegraphed an urgent message to his wife: "Upset Indians come pouring in. Please pray for us."

The next day when the rescue crew and family went to the site, Piton and the other missionaries were all found dead. They were trying to share the Gospel with Indians, but they were all killed. The missionary wives in their twenties cried out, holding onto the bodies of their dead husbands. Now they all became widows.

However, as the Holy Spirit came to those weak widows, what happened to them? Each one of them spoke in agreement. "We will complete the tasks that our husbands have not accomplished."

They made a big decision, moved into the Indian village, and shared the Gospel with the Indians. About forty years later, the whole village believed in Jesus as their savior. More astounding is the fact that the five Indians who murdered the missionaries all became Christians.

God's work is like this. God is pleased to raise the weak and use them as leading characters for His Kingdom. As I am getting weaker, the Lord considers me more preciously, and He pays attention to me from the throne in heaven and wants to empower me with His power. When the Holy Spirit comes upon such a weak one, the person can be used like Moody as a world-wide revivalist, and if the Holy Spirit comes upon even a small church in a mountain village, the church can be used for evangelization of this nation and this country.

Because I trust this fact, as I am getting older, my expectation is getting higher. As time passes and my body weakens more, I have bigger dreams that God will accomplish world evangelization through me because I am getting weaker, but the Lord is strong.

Are you downcast? Then I expect you to hold onto the Lord. I hope you hold to the Church. God will show you the most of His power through such a weak and insufficient person like you. God will surely make us sing the song of victory in the end. We are God's Church, and the Church of God is guaranteed to have the victory.

CPSIA information can be obtained
at www.ICGtesting.com
Printed in the USA
LVOW01s0801220716

497299LV00002B/2/P